Praise for "In One Piece a step by step guide to surviving change"

In One Piece – A step by step guide to surviving change, is a pragmatic, hands on guide perfect for anyone embarking on a change journey. Much like Mary-Beth herself, the book is down-to-earth, realistic yet aspirational and genuinely helpful. Full of practical tips and diverse real-world examples spanning multiple industries, *In One Piece*, is a well-crafted and engaging guide on how to not just survive, but thrive, through change.

Jane Hoban
Marketing Director – Specsavers Pty Ltd

Mary-Beth Hosking reminds us that the job of a leader is to produce sustainable change. Of course, everyone says they love change until it affects them personally. Mary-Beth has compiled valuable insights from her experience with change programs. She knows that the key to success is winning the hearts and minds of people around you. "In One Piece," is a leader's guidebook for producing game-changing results.

Brian Donovan
Director – Donovan Leadership

As a leader in technology, Mary-Beth is well-placed to talk about change. After all, technology often drives change for the benefit of an organisation. The hardest part of change is managing the human side, and Mary-Beth has that knowledge in spades too. A must read for any leader needing to guide their team through change, big or small.

Caroline Stainkamph - Director and Program Lead – The importance of Women in IT Vic ICT for Women

The change survival guide, *In One Piece*, provides practical advice, a robust reference list and real-life examples from the front lines of organisational change. If you are about to rollout changes across your business, this book can help you consider the details and nuances required to make the changes effective. Bring all the pieces of your 'business puzzle' into one piece with this book from Mary-Beth Hosking.

Temre Green | MSc, PhD
Executive Leader | Customer-Driven Results | Business
Transformation

If you are leading a team through change, reading this book will make you feel like someone has just put their arm around your shoulder and said, "*it's going to be alright*". Mary-Beth provides supportive and practical insights not only into what you need to do during change, but also how to be a great leader through the process.

Narelle Stevens
Former Operations Manager, Kearney

In
One
Piece

COMMUNICATION

KEEPING THE LIGHTS ON

TRANSITION & FRESH START

THE TRANSFORMATION FOUNDATION

WELLBEING

RESTRUCTURE

A step by step guide to surviving change

MARY-BETH HOSKING

First published in 2020 by Quantum Transformation | Melbourne

ISBN: 978-0-6489006-0-3

A catalogue record for this book is available from the National Library of Australia

Typeset, printed and bound in Australia by BookPOD

NATIONAL LIBRARY OF AUSTRALIA

A catalogue record for this book is available from the National Library of Australia

About the Author

Mary-Beth Hosking is a pragmatic and seasoned technology leader with extensive experience in organisational transformations. Mary-Beth holds a Master's Degree in Business and Technology with majors in Strategic management and Change management with over 20 years' experience leading restructures in multinational organisations.

Mary-Beth aspires to help leaders find a successful pathway whilst supporting their teams. Clearly understanding the impact of poorly led transitions has put Mary-Beth on a mission to develop sustainable change leadership by building resilience through transformation. With extensive experience leading through multiple restructures, Mary-Beth has wanted to help others by providing key insight and strategies to drive continued performance.

Mary-Beth acts as mentor, coach and trainer to those in the midst of organisational uncertainty. With a background in Business Change Management she has successfully delivered major programs during significant change and believes that by supporting leaders with practical tips and guidance they will be better equipped to manage through transitions ensuring overall well-being and continued productivity.

The author would like to thank Amanda Blesing for her guidance, Narelle Stevens for her diligent and exceptional editing skills and her husband Stuart for his continued support.

For additional information on the services Mary-Beth provides please see: quantumtransformation.com.au

Contents

Foreword

If you are reading this book, it is likely you are in the midst of, or about to embark on, a major organisational transformation. The purpose of this book is to provide leaders with pragmatic, proven guidance. Many of the ideas are not new, simply gathered and organised to help you lead your team through the change process.

I started this book several years ago when undertaking a major transformation in my own organisation. I found it hard to continue to guide my team under the pressure of change. I forgot some of the basics which would have helped us all. So, I began researching and compiling reference materials on how leaders can continue to deliver business imperatives, support their team and ensure their own well-being during change. Now, after leading many change programs, I have translated my learnings into this book.

Change permeates everything we do. How we navigate change reveals the type of leaders we are. Leaders are expected to have all the answers, know exactly what is going on and have the required tools. This may not be the case; we may be as much in the dark as our employees. How do you communicate with clarity? Leaders are also expected to enable their teams. This is challenging during major change particularly when the change is protracted, and your team is suffering from change fatigue. How do you keep your team motivated and productive? These questions will be addressed in this book, no matter where you are in the change cycle.

In this book we will focus on the 6 pieces of the change puzzle you will need to position correctly to emerge from the change journey in one piece. Each chapter will include useful tips and tools you can draw upon during any change that you may be embarking on. The model we are using is not linear because in practice change is not linear. You will need to consider some pieces then revisit them again, leave some pieces to the side and go back to them when it makes sense to do so.

Throughout the book I share suggestions and examples from my personal experience which I hope you find helpful.

Introduction

As a leader, there will come a time when you will be faced with change. For some it may be a small restructure, for others a larger more strategic change such as a new CEO, and others a complete transformation upon which the organisation's survival depends.

During any change it is important for leaders to remain focused on the future state of the organisation. You need to be a calming influence, a mentor and a coach. Your team depends on it and your organisation expects it.

Change can be seen as a "special" activity. But in today's world, change is continuous. Without continuous change and improvement organisations will fail. When individuals are impacted by major transformation, they may become resistant to change. Change is uncertain and with it brings fear. Individuals within your team may seek the predictable and gravitate to the known. It is our role as leaders to help our team's journey from the familiar safe place of the current organisation to the challenging, exciting and hopefully prosperous future organisation.

Navigating this journey is like completing a puzzle—understanding the size and shape of each of 6 key pieces—moving them and positioning them until they form a new whole.

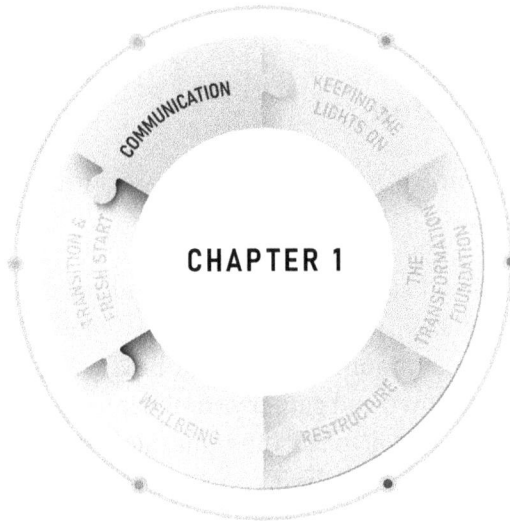

CHAPTER 1

The Communications Piece

Whatever the nature and size of the change you are involved in, communication is a critical piece of the change puzzle. Change related communication will likely start with a change announcement, move through a period of progress updates and finish with reflection and lessons learned. As a manager, communication with your team will be both in group meetings and one-on-one.

The change announcement

The change announcement is when either you as a leader, sometimes at the same time as your team, or sometimes in advance of your team, will be advised of the change by your organisation's senior leadership. It will impact you and your team. It will bring uncertainty. It may be perceived by you and your team positively or negatively. Regardless it represents the beginning of your important work as a communicator with your team.

What should you do when this happens?

Gather information

Knowledge is power—never more so than during organisational change!

The first step when dealing with a change announcement is to listen carefully to what has really been said. It is vital to remain calm. When changes are announced there can be a tendency to jump to conclusions. Slow down and gather as much information as possible. The best way to do this is to ask the right questions and get the best answers so you arrive at the best conclusions and be well placed to provide clear and accurate information to your team[1].

The four key types of questions as examined in the Harvard Business Review, to ask during times of change to help tease out the information you require are:

"Clarifying questions"[2] which help us clearly understand what has been stated. They are typically open questions such as "Can you tell me more?" or "Why do you think so?". Often people do not ask these questions, rather, make assumptions and fill in the blanks. During a major change you cannot afford to make assumptions as a leader. You must seek clarity.

✏️ Examples of Clarifying Questions:

While I was working at a large transportation company, the organisation announced a major restructure. The announcement came from the office of the Managing Director stating that due to company profits being much lower than expected there would be a major overhaul of the company structure.

As I was uncertain of what this change would mean to my team, I had many questions that needed answers and I needed to ask these of my line manager.

I asked the following questions:

Q: Can you tell me more about the change and what we can expect in the coming months?

Q: What does this mean for the project that my team is currently working on?

Q: What will this change mean to the roles of individuals in my team?

Q: What will this change mean for my role?

Q: Do we have a clear view of the timing of the changes?

"Adjoining questions"[3] are used to understand how related or surrounding parts of the organisation will be impacted by the change. For example, "How would this apply in a different context?" or "If we make this change which other departments will be affected by it?" It is tempting to focus on what our immediate actions need to be, rather than spend time asking exploratory questions. However, the more broadly we understand the change the more likely we are to focus on the right actions.

Examples of Adjoining Questions:

Q: If the outcomes of this change mean we need to reduce team size, how will we complete our main project? How many people am I expected to lose?

Q: If our main project is not completed it will affect the service team and the operations team. How will the business manage if we cannot deliver it?

Q: This project is designed to improve overall operational efficiency. If we cannot complete it other departments will be significantly impacted. What is expected in relation to this project?

Q: What are the key components of the project that need to be completed to cause the least impact on the organisation?

"Funnelling questions"[4] are used to provide a granular view. We ask these to understand how an answer was reached, to challenge assumptions, and to explore the root causes of problems. For example, "How was this analysis done?" or "When researching the solution, did we look at what other companies have done in this situation?" Gaining a deeper view of the change at hand will enable you to communicate with your team from a well-informed position.

📝 Examples of Funnelling Questions:

Q: I understand that I am being asked to reduce team size to achieve organisational goals, but this will inevitably impact the team's ability to deliver this main project. How were the numbers calculated for our department? What was the rationale to reduce my team size when we are part way through a primary project? Is it possible to discuss this decision with senior management to explain the impact that this reduction will have on the project and the broader business?

Q: Do I have any options other than team size reduction to achieve the organisational requirements? Can we discuss salary reduction, job share or other cost saving measures which would have a lesser impact?

"Elevating questions"[5] explore the broader issues and the big picture. Being too close to the change can lead to myopia. For example, "Taking a step back, what are the larger issues that this change will address?" Elevating questions help you to understand the strategic nature of the change.

Examples of Elevating Questions:

Q: Would you agree that IT is fundamental to both service delivery and overhead reduction in transport companies?

Q: How should IT managers being asked to reduce team size reconcile with that?

Q: What actions, other than reducing overheads, is the business considering?

Q: Can we look at efficiencies other than headcount reduction to improve the bottom line?

As you gather information through questioning and listening—be aware that there will be information that you may not be able to share with your team. At any point in time ensure you understand what is confidential and what can be shared.

The big "why"

It is critical that you understand why the change is taking place. In all your communications with your team the "why" comes before the "what" and the "how". If you have asked good questions like those set out in the examples above, you should be confident that you deeply understand the reason your organisation is embarking on the change. If the reason for the change is not clear to you, how will you make it clear to your team? As a leader your team's eyes will be on you—they will ask you why the change is necessary. If you do a convincing job of explaining "why" to your team—they are more likely to engage in the change process and be ready to join you on the journey.

"The Big Why" Example

"The transport industry is being commoditised. Customers are not interested in relationships with transport companies. They are looking for the cheapest option to move freight. Tracking and visibility are no longer a value add but an expected part of the service. Transport companies need to be smarter about the way in which they provide service and make operational efficiencies to reduce overheads at the same time.

Our company is buckling under the pressures of commoditised services, extensive overheads from large facilities and loss of revenue to new competitors in the market. This combined with some operational inefficiencies and lack of cohesive technology solutions across the business means we are no longer cost effective.

We can't continue operating in this way and have to make some major changes. This will mean reducing costs and overheads and improving operational efficiency. Some of the efficiencies we will focus on will include truck turn-around times when in depot, improved put-away processes in our warehouses and reduction of manual data key entry across our business units. Without these measures being put in place the business will not survive. Decisions need to be made that will be unpopular and will impact a significant number of people but without these there will not be a business at all."

Another "Big Why" Example

"Business is globalising. Many enterprises that have obtained a major market share in their home markets, must look to international markets if they seek growth. These global businesses will choose to work with advisers that also operate globally, so they can be supported around the world by one team who understands their businesses.

All of you are aware that our geographic strengths lie in the US and Asia, including Australia and New Zealand. We cannot compete with other firms who have a strong presence in Europe and the Middle East. Over the last several months we have lost 2 major accounts to competitors who are stronger than us in those geographies.

We are excited to advise that we have signed a Memorandum of Understanding to merge our operations globally with XYZ. This will mean firstly each country operation will merge locally and some duplicated jobs may be lost. At this stage, I cannot tell you which ones, but this information will be announced separately as soon as possible.

On the positive side for those who are interested, there may be opportunities to work internationally where the merged country units believe they still do not have the skilled resources to pursue business from large companies in those markets. Again, these opportunities will be communicated separately as soon as they become clear.

At this stage, for us here, it is business as usual, but there will be numerous changes down the track as we merge different teams and processes.

We would like each of you to discuss this with your team. We have set aside some time now for you to ask questions so that you feel you have the information you need."

Plan your communication

The fear and freneticism of change can become all-consuming and has the potential to derail your communication. We have all seen leaders caught on the spot and unable to answer questions they should be able to. You can avoid this by arming yourself with the information you have gathered and preparing to communicate it effectively. People will want to know what the change means for them as individuals. Answering their questions clearly is the only way to reduce the fear that will have been building since the change announcement.

The key to effective communication during change is small bites of information, kept simple, delivered at the right time. The best way to achieve this is to prepare a communication plan.

There are many communication plan templates available and I urge you to find one that suits you. Regardless of the template you use, it is important to be clear on your message, how you will communicate it, to whom and when. Here is a simple communication plan template that I have used before.

When building your communication plan Walker et al[6]. (2007) suggests covering the following five key areas:

1. Provide an explanation of gap between the As-Is state of the organisation and the To-Be state[7].
2. Show how the change will bridge the gap between As-Is and To-Be states[8].
3. Express assurance in the team's ability to effectively implement the change[9].
4. Demonstrate that the organisations leaders are behind the change[10].
5. Link the organisational change to personal benefits for your team[11].

QUANTUM TRANSFORMATION
Mentoring | Coaching | Change Advocacy

COMMUNICATION PLAN

Step	Who is my audience?	What is the purpose of this communication? What is the message?	What is my supporting material?	Who is the owner?	Target Date	Status	Comments/Learning/ Assessment of Effectiveness
1	Team Leads	Purpose: To advise of the changes Message: Reiterate the need to continue to deliver on the inflight projects	Change plans as provided by change champions	Manager	1/01/2020	In progress	Deliverables still on target
2	My Team	Purpose: To provide continued information on the change Message: Reiterate the need for the change in alignment with the overall business strategy	Change plans as provided by change champions	Manager	1/01/2020	In progress	Need to work with smaller teams and develop individual communications for them
3							
4							
5							
6							
7							
8							
9							
10							

Example:

Having shared "The Big Why" with my team, I turned my attention to ensuring that I covered the 5 points above as well.

We were a small department, compared to others. We were working on a project with finite deliverables and time frames. This meant that in the To-Be state there would not be a need for the department at all. This was a sobering message to deliver to the team.

I needed to focus on bridging the gap between the As-Is and what would happen to the team in the To-Be state. For some that would mean being moved on and for others they would be mobilised in different areas of the business. Our gap was simply to deliver the project to its completion so that the business would have the benefit of using the final product.

The change we were delivering was a significant uplift of the primary transport system for the business and was necessary to continue to deliver value to the customer base. The team would be required to deliver the project in the short term and some of them would be retained to continue to support the business. As they were experts in their fields they were assured of roles for the duration of the project.

I needed to emphasise that the organisation was committed to the team delivering the project, even during major upheaval. The investment to date had been significant and the business knew that without the delivery of the solution the business would struggle to effectively service the customer base.

Although for many of my team, I could not promise that they would be retained I worked with them to understand the benefits of completing the project to their ability to gain worthwhile employment either within other areas of the organisation, or in another organisation. The project, at the time, was using cutting edge technology and was enabling each employee to become highly sought after in the job market.

My focus was to keep my team engaged in completing the project by helping them see the benefits of staying until the project was delivered.

Your organisation's senior leadership should keep you updated along the change journey. You must communicate these updates to your team. Plan to keep your team as informed as possible—make sure they don't feel in the dark. This will require that you continually update your communication plan. Assess the outcomes that you expect to see from each communication activity and change the message, channel or frequency in order to achieve your communication goals. This is an instinctive process and you will need to be flexible. Some messages may fall flat but don't become discouraged. Remember that change is disruptive and when you communicate some people will hear what they want to hear. If it feels like your message has not hit the right spot—rephrase, simplify and repeat.

Communicate with positive language

Consciously adopt a positive approach to your communications. Positivity means being part of the solution and demonstrating openness and flexibility[12]. A positive approach can be contagious— if you are positive your team will likely be positive. According to Judge, Thoresen, Pucik and Welbourne, when a leader demonstrates positive behaviours, teams exhibit positive coping strategies which in turn alleviates some of the stress associated with change[13]. Your positivity about the change will strengthen the relationship you have with your team members—no one wants to work for a negative boss.

Ensure that the language you use helps to reinforce the positive nature of the change. Use positive language to frame the change in terms of tangible outcomes. Find a word picture of a To-Be state that resonates for you individually. Remain focussed on this picture when engaging with your team. This will help you to come across authentically and honestly and will assist to embed a positive message with your team.

Your team's engagement and productivity will be influenced by your words and actions. Lead through consistent messages and actions. Describing something differently each time you speak with your team will undermine their confidence that you have a clear picture of the future.

As leaders we are human, and it is entirely possible that we have our own insecurities to contend with. We may have experienced failed changes in the past and this may be tainting our own views of the changes ahead and influencing our word selection. If this is the case, it is even more critical that you plan your communications. It is easy for negative comments to creep in when communications are unplanned. The language you use should affirm the organisation's ability to prosper during and after the change. Remember it takes a lot of positive comments to counter a negative comment. Easier to avoid making them in the first place!

Debunk rumours

Change will bring a certain amount of hearsay and leaders must address it quickly. In a study by DiFonzo in 2009[14], "rumours can undermine the need for change". Rumours will not help your team and will hinder their ability to deliver. If individuals become focussed on false information their productivity will decline. This may in turn generate dissatisfaction across the team and the organisation. The rule of thumb is simple, if it does not come from legitimate leadership, then debunk it. Your role as leader is to ensure your team has the best available information. Circumventing rumours may feel like a fulltime job during a change—but it is so important. Be sure to include addressing rumours in your communication plan.

Example:

Continuing the transport company case— there was a lot of conflicting information that was not coming from official channels. I would find myself coming to the office each day and having to put out small "fires" based on rumours and lunchroom conversations. Not only did this create additional work for me but it also created emotional reactions from my team members.

In this instance I spoke directly with the HR director to gain a clear understanding of what was happening, the change process that the business was planning to follow and the information I was allowed to share. I pulled together a communication plan which set out timelines based on what the team was expected to deliver during the change and where possible exactly what the organisation was planning.

When asked specific questions I answered with the information I had gathered and did not volunteer more than was available. I did not speculate on what I thought may happen as this would have created greater emotional distress to my team members. Curating the communications based on fact allowed me to respond to rumours with the facts which established a basis of trust with my team.

Some of the rumours that were circulating were the potential outsourcing of the technology function. At the time of the change announcement there was no discussion about outsourcing and I needed to spend considerable time reassuring team members that roles would not be outsourced during the build phase of the project.

The more serious "fires" I needed to put out were team members actively looking outside of the organisation for roles whilst they were still needed to deliver the project. I worked with my key team members and assured them that when the project was coming to a close, I would work with them to assist in getting roles either outside of the organisation or somewhere within it.

The rumours became harder to manage as the business started to reduce team sizes and let people go. These retrenchments were not announced. When people tried to contact someone, they would find out that they had been let go and whatever work they may have been doing may not get done. This caused a lot of angst for my team as they did not even have the opportunity to say goodbye and therefore it sparked fear and loss and impacted delivery.

Example:

Continuing the global services example — there were rumours that all country back office functions were going to be centralised into one hub based in India. Several people had approached their managers in tears saying that they did not want to lose their jobs.

At this point I was unaware of any such plan, in fact back office teams had not been discussed. I decided to check this with the Managing Director. She told me that the organisation was not even close to considering back office teams, the merger integration committee would be totally focussed on merging the professional services teams around the world first—to ensure that client work was not disrupted. This would be the focus for at least the first year of the merged organisation.

When I spoke with my team, I shared the information that I was provided, I did not speculate on anything that may or may not happen to back office teams in the future. I made it clear that for now their role was business as usual and to do everything they could to support the client services teams with anything extra they needed while transitioning into their new teams.

Engage early with individuals

As a leader navigating change you must communicate one-on-one where possible with team members[15]. If this is not possible then break the team down into logical groups. Ensure this engagement comes early as in itself it will be an intervention that may help you to address any negative impacts of the change. It will also help you to gain a clear understanding of what your team members are thinking and feeling. Gauging their sentiment will provide insight into your team's ability to continue to deliver.

Engagement with you will provide your team members with a voice and an opportunity to express their views about the change in a safe space. The simple act of actively listening to each team member or small group will protect and build a strong culture of trust. In addition, it will provide you with a view as to those in the team who may become your ongoing change advocates and those who might slip into underperformance.

Change Advocate Example

I have been fortunate to have worked with change advocates who clearly understood the need for change and were willing to assist me to make the change happen.

On one occasion I was required to change the entire structure of a department. This restructure did not involve letting team members go but it did change structures and reporting lines for most of the individuals concerned. I needed the support of someone who understood why the change was necessary and could explain it to their peers.

One person in my team stood out. She had been in the business for quite some time and had built up strong relationships across the department. I asked her to help me deliver the change message to clusters of individuals to ensure the message was clearly understood.

When there were concerns with some of the team, my change advocate would raise them with me and help me work with people on an individual level. This approach ensured that very few people left the organisation due to the change, and those that stayed had a clear view of the change in the language they would understand.

Have open and honest conversations with the team members most impacted by the change to understand where they see themselves. You will find that some individuals are not interested in being part of the future organisation and want to look at other opportunities. There will be individuals who may not have the capability to transition and you will need to work with them on the best options for their futures. These are difficult conversations to have and they will need to take place relatively quickly. The key is to be honest with your team members and make sure they have as much information as you can share so that they can begin to think about their own future within or without the organisation.

Example:

After discussing the global services merger with my team, I had a staff member approach me with some concerns. He explained to me that he had joined our firm because he wanted to work for a small firm where people were not treated as a number. In addition, he was not interested in being part of international client service teams where significant amounts of travel was required.

We had a long, open discussion where I agreed with him that the merged firm would be much larger and there was no doubt that international travel would increase. We agreed that he was probably best to look for a role in a smaller, local firm and I agreed to help him do so.

I expect this openness and support will result on a long-term advocate for our firm.

Marketing the change

Your organisation's senior leadership will expect you to positively market the change to your team on an ongoing basis. It is likely that you have regular team meetings already in place and you should use them to keep your team updated on the progress of the change. Senior leadership are likely to have their own communications strategy and may even issue you with "packs" of information to use with your team to market the change. Ensure that the language you use aligns with the overall change message, while it can be nuanced to suit your team, the message needs to be consistent. Work with any change champions that may have been appointed by senior leadership to validate your message and ensure there are no ambiguities or inconsistencies.

Example:

The entire organisation was undertaking a major transformation due to increasing market pressures.

The corporate message was:
"In order to survive we need to reduce costs, increase services and improve efficiency"

My message to the team was:
"To support the business, we need to continue to deliver value. To do this we must complete our project so the business can work efficiently without extensive manual intervention. This will improve overall efficiency and help the organisation to reduce costs and improve services."

Your own communications plan, tailored to the needs and style of your team, is the vehicle for planning how you communicate the organisation's messages along with your own to your team.

Clarity of message and understanding the change are two of the superordinate themes in this book. Keep returning to these principles when communicating with your team. Clarity brings a sense of comfort and preserves and builds team buy-in. Without clarity it is hard to stave off rumours and to keep your team aligned to the broader vision. As the work of change gets done, you will develop clearer insight into how processes and structures will change, how the future state organisation will look. You need to share this picture with your team.

Negativity as a result of change history

How many times have you heard people say *"I have seen this organisation try to change before and that failed, therefore this will fail too"* or *"Every major change project has failed so what makes this one any different. Big changes always fail"*? These are examples of anchoring and this a key concept to understand and address when leading and communicating through change[16]. When you are working towards a future direction, having individuals use previous experiences to bring a negative commentary to the change will be detrimental.

Anchoring is the act of using an initial piece of information to make subsequent judgments[17]. We start with something we are sure of and then make assumptions (if somewhat calculated assumptions) from there. Anchors can have a positive or negative effect. When the effect is negative, they need to be addressed.

Here is how you might address negative anchoring in a team meeting:

"I am aware that you have been through a change like this in the past and it wasn't a great success"

It is important to be open and honest about why the change was unsuccessful: "This was due to...".

Then reflect on the upcoming process and be open and honest about why you think it will be different. "However, I really believe this change will succeed because...."

———— ••• ————

One change I was involved in was where a significant function was being outsourced to an offshore vendor. The conversation went something like this:

"I am aware that when we attempted to outsource the development of a key function within our freight management system it wasn't a great success. This was because we did not have a clear understanding of the customer requirement nor did we have a well-developed vendor engagement process in place.

However, we have taken the lessons learnt from that experience and now have a solid vendor engagement process in place. We have engaged experts to ensure that we do not run into the same problems. In addition, we will take it slowly with offshoring so that we build a better understanding of working with offshore vendors."

Research your organisation's change history. Typically, there will be some events that have given rise to negative assumptions[18]. Lead with authenticity and create an environment where you have open discussions about previous situations and perceived failures.

Establish rapport by sharing some of the anchors you have battled with in the past.

Where an organisation has had multiple unsuccessful change efforts, there may be a higher level of distrust amongst the team[19]. Understanding and discussing the organisation's change history is an important part of marketing the change to your team[20].

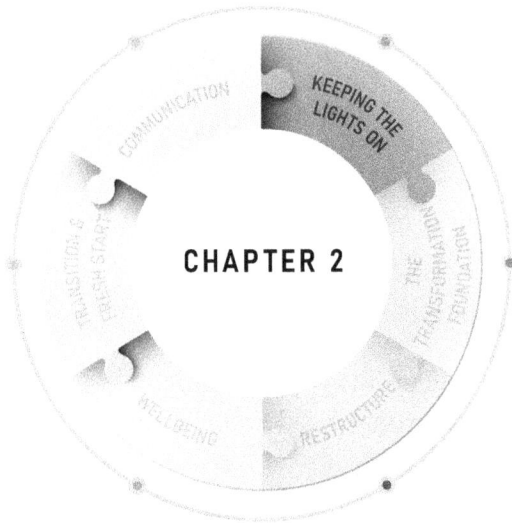

CHAPTER 2

Keeping the Lights On

Keeping the lights on means continuing to deliver whilst the change is underway. If change management is about persuading people to break with the status quo[1] and embrace a different approach to their work, then how do they continue to deliver when their world is changing around them? You may be asking them to continue doing something enthusiastically that will cease to be required in the To-Be state of the organisation.

As leaders we are meant to steer through change and keep the team productive. Change in any form is disruptive and can cause heightened emotions—as a leader you must remain poised and not get emotional yourself.

Be clear on responsibilities

There is a chance that you and your team may be an integral part of the change implementation—in other words, doing change related work. Alternatively, or in parallel, you may remain responsible for ensuring your team's business as usual or current organisation work. If necessary, speak to your organisation's leadership to be clear about you and your team's role during the change. You must be in no doubt what you and your team are responsible for delivering.

Be a sound decision maker

During change you may find yourself thinking instinctively and using your "gut feel" when making decisions. This works well in short bursts when operating in familiar territory. However, when we are dealing with prolonged or complex organisational change situations, you may find this approach exposes you to erratic decisions. Rather, you need to be thinking deliberately and taking the time to make well thought out decisions. Your team will keep working well for you if they see you making sound decisions.

"Thinking Fast and Slow" by Daniel Kahneman[2] and "The Art of Thinking" by Rolf Dobelli[3] have helped me understand the way in which people think—how we come to decisions and how we draw conclusions based on our own cognitive biases and anchors.

In "Thinking Fast and Slow" the concept of having two distinct ways of thinking is explored—the way in which the two work together help with decision making during organisational change.

As described by Kahneman[4] there are two systems of thought:

- "System 1 is the automatic response"[5]
- "System 2 is the effortful response"[6]

"System 1 is generally used when you are making routine decisions"[7]. This will help you when you have multiple queries or actions that need to take place. This is the thinking you do for your standard day to day activities. This is where you will draw on your past experiences and underpinning biases or anchors. Issues that you know how to respond to because you have responded to them many times before.

"System 2 is used when you need to address issues with more effort and attention"[8]. This is where you are drawing new conclusions based on available information at a given time. A change where there are multiple unknowns will require greater thought and attention and the need to use System 2 will become present[9].

Although you use both types of thinking, finding the balance between your automatic responses and your effortful[10] responses are necessary during a change. As system 1 uses your learned responses, biases and anchors[11], it is important to continue to gather information in order to challenge whether reliance on previous experiences is valid. If you are over relying on biases and learned behaviours, it may be affecting the quality of your responses during the change. If this is happening to you, then it is highly likely to be happening to your team as well.

To ensure that you are thinking deliberately, use the process of gathering information and planning your actions to ensure that you are not making instinctive decisions.

Thinking fast and thinking slow in action

These days when I am hired into organisations it is because I have a proven record of managing teams through organisational change. Having managed many changes throughout my career, I have a process that works and enables my team to come through changes reasonably unscathed. I do this by drawing on my previous experiences and adapting as the change dictates. Not all changes are the same and some do require modifications to my standard approach.

However, when I embarked on my very first change, my approach was very different to what it is now. Every step of the change required a great deal of thought and preparation. I needed to look at all elements deliberately and be certain about my approaches in every aspect of the change.

I was new to organisational change and I was not sure of what steps I needed to take. Every communication took hours to write and multiple iterations. I found myself having to review everything I said to ensure that what I was communicating would not create repercussions across the team.

In my very first change, I knew that people would be retrenched but was not allowed to mention this. I knew that the group I worked for would be shut down and that people would be displaced but I could not discuss this. I was not able to make decisions rapidly as all of the changes taking place were new for me. I was thinking about communications and the best way to take my team along for the journey but not having done this before it felt very laboured and challenging. The unknown of the change forced me to think slowly and learn what to do.

What I did know was how to do my job and keep my team focussed on their current roles. For me thinking fast was keeping my team engaged in the tasks they knew how to do. I could make rapid decisions based on the work that we had been doing. I would make decisions on continuing to support the business as we had been and there was no need to alter this.

After many changes I have learnt a lot. I draw on this experience automatically so when a change is triggered by the change announcement, I know exactly what I need to do and say and without hesitation I embark on a well-honed process.

For me this is the difference between thinking fast and slow[12].

Link positivity to actions

Your senior leadership will likely be encouraging you to celebrate quick wins[13]. This is a standard practice to build momentum during a change. However, be careful to celebrate those actions you want people to remain focussed on.

Try to find ways of linking the celebration of quick wins to positive team outcomes. It is likely your team has existing measures of success such as customer satisfaction scores, sales results or reduced downtime. Linking a win, such as successfully adopting a new system, to a positive change in those targets will demonstrate that the change will make it easier for the team to achieve their objectives in the future.

When wins are being celebrated by the broader organisation—for example, successful completion of a pilot program—ensure you point out the input your team has made to that success. Not only will this create pride in their contribution but may also help to shift any negative thoughts that may be affecting them.

As quick wins are recognised and celebrated, the team will become more invested in the changes and will want to see them through. Once the change is complete, they will also want to ensure that the changes are adhered to[14].

How many times have you tried to lose weight? I know that this is not exactly the type of case study that you would expect when thinking about organisational change but when we embark on a personal change such as weight loss it is a fundamental change to our status quo.

Unless we have a health imperative to change, the chances are, if we don't see immediate results, we may lose momentum. If we embark on the change and in the first few weeks, we see quick results we feel good. We feel that the end goal is achievable, and we feel inspired to continue.

Then we get to a point where we have either plateaued or possibly gained weight. This is the moment we may give up. The change feels too hard to continue and we revert to our old habits.

When we feel like giving up, we may change the way we measure. We may stop focussing on weight loss and focus on girth loss which links a positive outcome to the change.

This happens with work changes as well. Unless we focus on the small wins along the change journey and look at ways of linking success to the change, it is possible that we will revert to our old ways of working and the change will fail.

Re-framing the change

During the change effort you may find team members struggling to remain focused on the tasks at hand. The change announcement may have left the team with a sense of uncertainty which may affect their focus on continuing to deliver. If this is happening it may help to return to the change announcement and deconstruct its message and re-frame it in a way that is meaningful to your team. As discussed by Dobelli if a message is communicated in different ways it will also be received in different ways[15].

"In a research study documented by Dobelli, participants were asked to choose the healthier option from these two:

- Option A: This new product is 99% fat free
- Option B: This new product has 1% fat

Participants selected option A even though the outcomes were the same. The way in which the message was framed made a difference to the participant response"[16].

This will be the same for your team. You know your team; you are in the best position to re-frame messages that will provide them with the information they need in a way they can consume without negatively impacting their delivery.

Example:

During a major change I was involved in, the message that was delivered went something like this:

> "The business is in financial trouble; the numbers are not good, and we need to make some drastic changes. We expect significant redundancies and have engaged an external party to assist us with the work ahead."

As a leader of a significant team, it was my job to ensure that the project we were completing was delivered before the inevitable happened. Framing the message to my team at the time was challenging. There were questions I could not answer and framing the message in a positive way was difficult. Here is what I put together:

> "I know that there is major change ahead and that we are all feeling uncertain. What we do know is that we have a project to complete and finite time within which to do it. I cannot promise you a role at the end of this project, but I will work with each of you to find other opportunities either within the group or externally. I am with you and together we will work through this as a team."

Although the message was the same, the framing came from letting the team know I was with them in this and together we would work through it. There is no way to make bad news better and it doesn't get better with time. Framing assists to make the message easier to digest but in the end, it is still the same message.

Guide with intent

When involved in a change, whether or not you are part of the leadership team that has instigated it, the most effective way to navigate it is to guide with intent. This means understanding the aim or plan and progressing towards it.

Be unwavering in your approach and articulate the change in terms of results for the organisation. Link this to how the team are assisting to make the change possible by focussing on the work they are currently doing. Use every opportunity to interact with your team to encourage them to challenge this linkage if they cannot see it. Answer what you can. Ensure that every word and action you use is thoroughly thought out, aligned and consistent.

Example:

In the previous example I talked about having to deliver a project for the organisation, knowing that it was entirely possible that most of the team would either be redeployed or retrenched. In this situation guiding with intent meant guiding with that outcome in mind. Goals and benefits needed to be short term in nature (for example, your bonus will be paid on delivery of the project). I could not promise anything in the longer term, so I needed to avoid references to people's involvement in future work in the organisation. However, I was always happy to share my view on jobs and opportunities people wanted to consider after the project delivery.

As leaders, we can only make decisions based on the information we have at any given time. However, we all know things can change and it is important to remain flexible. Should any change activity alter the work your team is required to do along the way, explain why and get your team headed off in the new direction. Use your communications plan to ensure that you are communicating authentically and openly with your team.

Prolonged change

When a change goes on for many years with multiple rounds of redundancies, structural change and a lack of an overall end point, your team may have lost trust in the organisation. They may have lost faith in you as their leader.

If this is the case—go back to basics. Get the team to focus on the job at hand, remember what they are in the organisation to achieve. Use reward and recognition of team and individual achievements to continue to recognise your team's good work.

Keep the lights on by focussing on delivery. Use your communication plan and keep the team as informed as possible. Try to ensure there is always an end point in sight.

Recently I was communicating with a colleague who was involved in a protracted change. She was struggling to keep her team engaged and she felt as though every communication with the team was received with great scepticism.

She asked me for my views on what she could be doing differently although she knew that the change would continue for a considerable time longer. I asked where she felt the business was in the change process and she said there were still significant changes, including more retrenchments to come.

I advised her that she needed to gain clarity once again and start asking the organisation's management direct questions about the expected timelines. Although she was in the midst of the change, she was going to have to go back to the start of the process.

I suggested that she needed to go back to basics with her communication plan, her understanding of what was to come and look to engage change advocates. She agreed that she needed to do this to rebuild the trust within the team.

As a leader there is nothing wrong with going back to basics and starting the process once again. Change is not linear and sometimes we have to start again and reinforce what we have learnt to date.

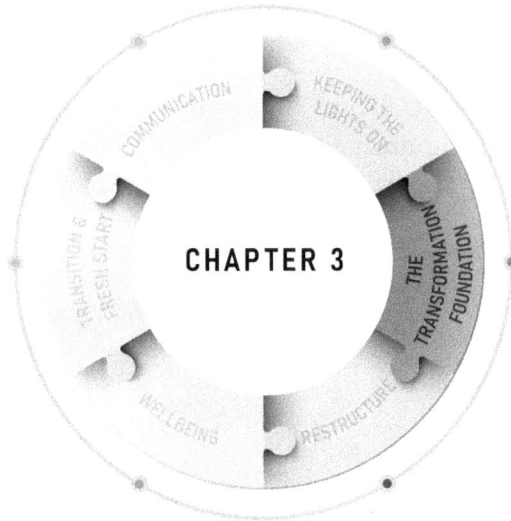

CHAPTER 3

The Transformation Foundation Piece

As a leader there will be three buckets of work you will need to juggle to make the transition effectively.

1. As-Is or "business as usual" tasks. This is the work you were doing as a team before the change was announced. Some or all of this may transition to the future organisation. Some of this may need to continue until the future state replacement work is ready to commence.

2. To-Be work. This is the work your team will be doing after the change is complete. You may take this on gradually as the future state organisation takes shape, or it may be quite abrupt if a function is completely retired and the team is given an entirely new focus. It might be similar to the As-Is work you were doing, or it might be quite different depending on the breadth and depth of the change.

3. Change work. These are the additional pieces of work that need to be done to transition the As-Is to the To-Be state. They have

a change-specific focus. This work typically starts when the change is being planned and wraps up after it has been fully transitioned. This work is the focus of this chapter.

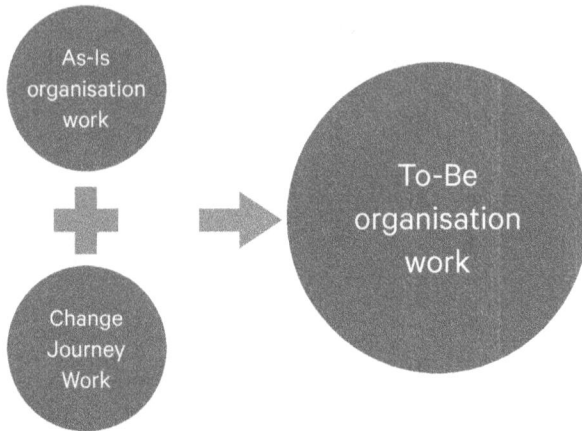

As-Is organisation work

+

Change Journey Work

To-Be organisation work

Work effectively with the change team

While change can be delivered top down where the change is enforced upon the organisation with a strategic imperative or bottom up where the change is organic—most often it will be a combination of both. A top down/bottom up approach is where the change is a strategic initiative, but tactical action takes place from the bottom up[1].

Typically, where a top down/bottom up approach is being pursued, senior leadership will form or hire a team of people to lead the transformation. Sometimes these people are referred to as "change champions". In addition, working groups may be formed to focus on tactical aspects of the change program. If there are working groups that you and your team can add value to—volunteer to lead or participate in one or two of them. Get in front of the decision makers and demonstrate the value that you and your team can bring. Leading working groups will enable you to put your own mark on the change and to guide the outcome. In addition, your involvement will show an openness to new experiences and an ability to adjust and cope with the change.

Example:

During one major transformation, the organisation I worked with brought on change consultants to assist with the change.

I proposed to my line manager, at the time, that I would like to be involved in the change work with the consultants as I felt that my team and I would be able to add value to the process. He agreed it would be a good idea to ensure that we were across the changes as they took place and had input into the change activities.

On this occasion, the change team were engaged to impose the change. Leaders were not invited to give their opinions on the changes—they were just told to implement them. This could be viewed negatively, and some people may not wish to work with a team taking that approach. However, I saw it as an opportunity. Although I could not impact the change schedule, I did know the schedule and what to expect and was able to communicate more accurately with my team.

Although at the outset it did not appear that I could influence any decisions—once I was working alongside the change team there were some decisions regarding resourcing that I was able to influence because it was clear to them that I knew the people within the organisation who could add value. This enabled me to act as an advocate for skilled people from within the change team. Although this may seem like a small thing, for those individuals impacted, it was very much appreciated.

During any major transformation that you are not leading, look for any opportunity to get close to the change decision makers so can learn about what is going on as early as possible and you may be surprised by how much influence you can have.

Whether you are leading a working group and/or your current state work team, expect to receive a lot of direction from the change champions throughout the change process. It is their role to keep the momentum going and it is critical that you work effectively with them.

Understand the change model

Change champions will typically be using a change model. If you have not had the opportunity to work through an organisational change before, this may feel new to you. Research the type of change model being used. This will enable you to speak the same language as the change champions and help you to understand where, in the change process, the organisation is. You will feel in more control and have a framework you can use to explain the change to your team.

There are several credible models the change champions may be using or modifying for your organisation. The well-known ones include (but are not limited to):

- Kotter's Change Management Theory[2]
- Lewin's Change Management Model[3]
- McKinsey 7S Model[4]
- ADKAR[5]

If you aren't already familiar with these models, try to get a high-level understanding of each one (time permitting). Speak with the change team and ask them about their change methodology—ask them to take you through it and explain how they plan to lead the change. Choose the model most similar to the one they are using and research it more deeply. Even if they do not have a specific model, ask them to take you through how they anticipate leading the change so that you know how best to work with them.

Kotter's Model is my preferred approach, but I do adapt it to suit the businesses I work with. These are the ideas from Kotter's model that I focus on:

- I spend a great deal of time understanding the impact of the change at the team, department, business and organisation levels.

- I spend time analysing the stakeholders who will be impacted by the change.
- Celebrate wins along the way. Calling out key contributors. These small things really help to keep team members engaged.
- Identify change advocates and change blockers early.
- Keeping a lessons learnt log to ensure when I am involved in another change I have information from previous changes to reflect upon

Get involved

There will be opportunities for you and your team to shine during the change process. Show a strong willingness for you and your team to get involved in the change work. Explain the future state the organisation is trying to achieve and help your team create goals which engage them and deliver outcomes the organisation values. There may be critical projects that are both highly visible and developmental—if your team has the right skill set, volunteer. Involvement and visibility will not only raise your profile but will elevate your team as well. It will display a maturity during change which will provide you with leverage in the future state organisation.

What do you do if you cannot see ways of getting involved? Remain focused on what you know your team needs to deliver. Keep displaying your team's value to the organisation throughout the change.

Get your team involved

When working with a major transportation company embarking on significant business changes, my Continuous Improvement (CI) team was asked to work with the change champions in order to embed new practices into the business. Not only were we expected to continue to deliver on our inflight CI projects but also to embed cost saving measures across the business and change processes that were designed to improve overall business performance.

I saw this as an opportunity for senior management to see my team in a positive light. Having Lean Six Sigma qualified team members it seemed a likely choice to have my team involved. Each team member worked on various aspects of the change and when the processes were bedded in, each of them was offered roles in the new structure.

The exposure that my team members had with the change champions and upper management meant that when specific roles within the new structure were being resourced, they were considered in the first instance. Although some of my team members were uncomfortable with the changes taking place, they were grateful when they were taken into the new structure and had greater opportunities open up for them.

Business process mapping and re-engineering

This is the critical process of changing the actual work your team does. Essentially it is re-engineering your As-Is business processes into the To-Be business processes and structure. Typically, your team will need to focus on As-Is tasks until it makes sense to transition to the To-Be state. You will be ahead of the curve if you already have your As-Is processes clearly documented—if you do not, this is work you will need to do.

The change champions may provide you with an organisational structure and To-Be process maps. If they do not—ask for them. You can then compare your As-Is processes and activities with the To-Be processes and activities and get a clear picture of how the work of your team will change.

If the organisation structure and To-Be process maps are not provided to you by the change team, you will need to prepare them yourself. You need to ensure all the To-Be processes have been clearly and completely mapped and that you understand them. Be certain to work with the change champions (or leadership) on this for your team—there must be one clear version of the truth. Gaps or inaccuracies in processes can make or break a team's ability to deliver.

Example:

Let's take a simple system change request process. Pre-change, this is what the high-level process map might have looked like.

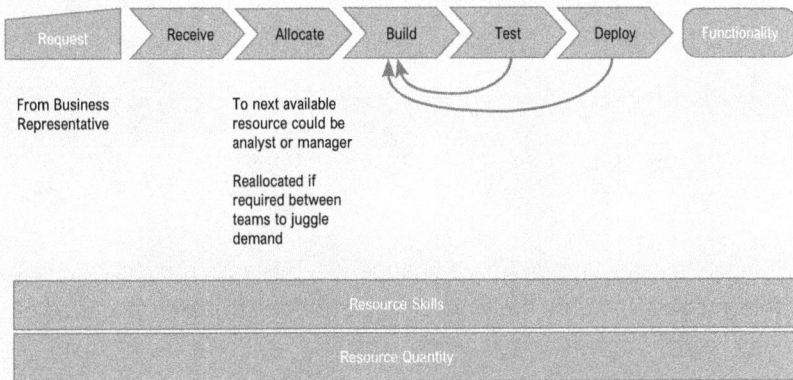

This process had served the organisation reasonably well for some time, but as the business grew there was pressure on support functions to become more productive and commercial. Some of the changes that were being requested by the business were:

- Increased triage and prioritisation—not all requests are urgent and or important to the business.

- Better communication between the function and the business representative so that inconsistencies in requirements could be captured before entering the build phase to reduce the amount of rework.
- The work be allocated to one team to see through rather than passed around between teams with little coordination.
- Improved quality assurance.

The new business process map looked like this.

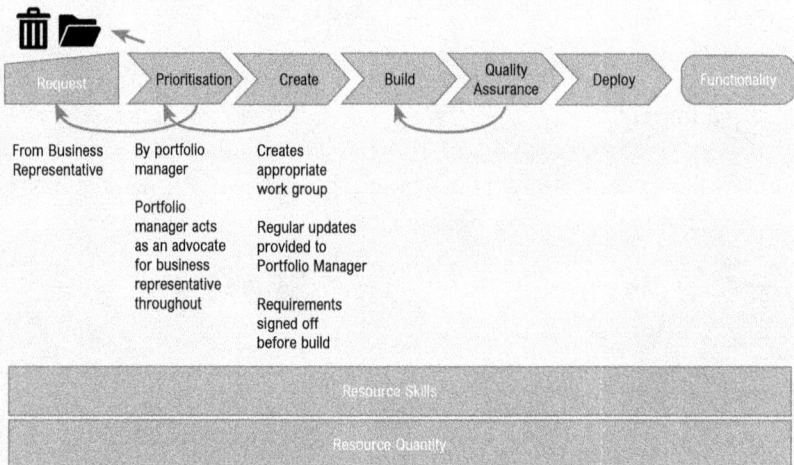

It is worth reflecting on how a change in a business process such as this impacts not only the work being done but the skills and size of your team:

- Not all requests are now accepted by the team at a point in time, so the number of units (requests) flowing through the process would be expected to decrease, perhaps allowing for quantity of resourcing to decrease.
- The Portfolio Manager's role changes significantly – from being primarily part of the build team to a prioritiser, team creator, and business communicator. Does the incumbent have the skills?

- Appropriately skilled teams do the work. This should allow for less generalisation and more specialisation of talent. Perhaps different staff, skills and likely improved quality.
- Emphasis moves from testing to quality assurance. Does the team have the skills?
- Iteration moves from re-work of solutions to agreement of requirements. Perhaps different skills and less man hours?

Upskill individuals

As your future state processes become clear, as seen from the previous example, you may find that some team members do not have the required skills. A good leader is alert for this and explores what can be done to bring all (or most) employees across to the future organisation. If there are skill gaps, you will need to consider upskilling the individuals involved.

Have open and honest conversations with the team members most impacted by the change to understand where they see themselves. You will find that some individuals are not interested in any upskilling on offer and want to look at other opportunities. There will be individuals who may not have the capability to upskill and you will need to work with them on the best options for their futures.

If team members' roles are redefined, new job or position descriptions will be required. The change champions may develop these together with Human Resources, or it may be the responsibility of each team leader. The new position descriptions along with your future state process maps should provide a clear view of tasks that are different to those that the team were performing. It is a logical next step to ask—do they have the knowledge and skills that will be required to perform those new tasks?

The best way to achieve a clear understanding of your team's capabilities is to complete a capability matrix. It helps leaders assess capabilities at a granular level. When you consider the capabilities collectively as one job, you will quickly get a picture of each incumbent's ability to meet the performance requirements of their new role within the new structure.

This also facilitates an understanding of where training is most needed. Training not only builds required capability but is an opportunity to build trust by showing your team that the organisation is willing to invest in them.

Team development

In addition to individual team member upskilling, you will need to work with your people as a group as they develop from a current state to a future state team. I have found Tuckman's stages of group development very useful[6]. There are tools that can be used at each stage of the model. These tools can be used separately or in unison depending on the maturity of the team. In my own team I have used all the tools and whenever there is a change to the team, no matter how small, I revisit them.

Mourning[7]

The first stage we will consider is the mourning stage[8]. This stage enables teams to break up and move on to form new teams. During change people leave a team and new people come on board. When your team is going through this, allow them time to mourn, to say goodbye to the past and be ready to embrace what the transformed organisation will become and what their new team will look like. Where possible celebrate the achievements of the past—many of your team will be proud of them. This is possibly the most important point for leaders to embrace the change themselves.

Mourning is not a fast process but if it is actioned with deliberate focus it will yield great results for the organisation and your team.

QUANTUM TRANSFORMATION
Mentoring | Coaching | Change Advocacy

CAPABILITY MATRIX

Role:

Person:

INDIVIDUAL

	Below what is required for role	Developing required competency	Appropriate for role	Above what is required for role	At next level
Business Communications			X		
Customer Service				X	
Influencing and Negotiating		X			
Innovation and Creativity			X		
Presentation Skills	X				

TEAM

Capabilities appropriate or above

	Person 1	Person 2	Person 3	Person 4	Person 5
Business Communications	X	X	X		
Customer Service	X	X	X		
Influencing and Negotiating		X	X	X	X
Innovation and Creativity		X	X	X	X
Presentation Skills	X				X

Example:

When working for an R&D business within a large company we were told that our division would be closing down. All employees were advised that they would be relocated into different divisions of the organisation. Although all roles would remain somewhere in the business, the division we were working in would no longer exist.

As the senior leadership team, we felt that it was important to celebrate the great work that had been achieved over the 8 years of the division's existence. We felt that we needed to give all employees closure and to thank them for the great work they had done. We wanted to give them a chance to celebrate and say goodbye. This was a way of mourning and grieving the change but embracing the future.

We put together a "Yearbook" similar to those you see in American graduations. We held a graduation party for all employees and encouraged everyone to sign each other's year books. We celebrated the wins and we mourned the losses. We provided all employees with closure in order for them to start fresh in their new roles.

Forming[9]

Forming is the next stage in Tuckman's model[10]. This is where team members learn about opportunities and challenges, where they create ground rules for working together and test boundaries for interpersonal and task behaviours[11]. During this stage you may notice that your team is not working as a cohesive unit. They may be working independently of each other. This is because some individuals will cling on to the old ways of working. Some may prematurely abandon existing tasks and dive into the new work. There could be an unhealthy tension across the team and significant frustrations may be aired. Although the team will be delivering, you may see a decrease in the quality and quantity of output. All these symptoms are telling you it is time to draw the new team together.

How do you start the process of forming the new team? It is helpful to discuss and agree the vision of your team. This will set the boundaries for the ways of working together discussion which will come later[12]. The power of a shared vision is to have the entire team involved in its development. As a leader you will have your view, but you must involve your team. You will need to make concessions regarding what you want and what they want. This is a powerful first step in bringing cohesion to the team.

📝 Example:

When working with a newly formed team I spend time observing the way in which the team functions. I spend time with each team member quizzing them on what works and what doesn't work. I work through the objectives that the team needs to meet in order to support the department's goals. I then document my observations of the team's behaviours (try to limit to 5), elaborate on the observations and present them to the newly formed team. We then brainstorm how we can improve the behaviours. This leads onto a discussion on what the shared vision for the department should be. For me having a shared vision enables me to start workshopping the ways of working based on the common goal.

Observations

QUANTUM TRANSFORMATION
Mentoring | Coaching | Change Advocacy

As a leader what have you observed about the team behaviours.
List here (try not to have more than 5)

1. Single point sensitivity
2. Blame mentality
3. Processes are not adhered to
4. Customer communications appear lacking
5. Our stakeholders do not understand our processes

Observations detailed

QUANTUM TRANSFORMATION
Mentoring | Coaching | Change Advocacy

Elaborate on the observations with a sentence for each.

6. I've observed that we have a lack of knowledge transfer across the team
7. Without robust processes and strict adherence our ability to deliver quality products and services are impacted
8. Without proven communication and implementation strategies we will not succeed in making changes stick
9. Without clearly defined stakeholder engagement our customer will become our adversary and not our partner

Vision

QUANTUM TRANSFORMATION
Mentoring | Coaching | Change Advocacy

Based on your observations what is our vision to improve the department.

For example:
Delivery will drive best practice in project management, quality and engagement across the our function.

We do this by ensuring process adherence, enabling continuous improvement, assuring quality, direct stakeholder engagement and celebrating our wins.

Storming[13]

The next stage in the Tuckman model is storming[14]. This is where you focus on the business process maps for the To-Be state organisation. Work through them in detail with your team. Encourage the team to discuss what they are comfortable with and what they want to challenge. Help them to understand what the organisation is asking them to "Stop, Start, Continue". Expect this review to drive robust discussion. This is a good thing—it will generate key learnings, ways of improving the processes along with a significant level of engagement and cohesion.

In addition, it will help to build on your positive team culture by encouraging individuals to develop recommendations and experiment with new ways of working. Try to ensure that each team member has a say. If you are actively listening and taking on board what your team is saying you will gain insight into team members who may be a flight risk *("I am not doing that")* and those who will become your change advocates *("I am keen to give that a try")*.

Allow your team members to voice their concerns and opinions and share what they feel will help the team. Do not discount what they have to say. As a leader you need to be consistently and actively listening to your team. There will be a lot of noise and emotion you will need to sift through but in amongst it there will be some gems that will enhance and improve your ways of working.

Example:

When working with my teams on our ways of working I like to bring the entire department together (if possible, based on size) to work through our processes. This is performed as an open forum where everyone is invited to write down which processes and behaviours should Stop, Start or Continue.

Appoint a facilitator for the session if you can—they should ensure times are adhered to and bring themes together in an unbiased way.

What you will need:

- A room large enough for the entire group
- Spare wall space and brown butchers' paper on 3 of the 4 walls
- Multiple pads of post it notes
- Plenty of pens

- Bluetac if needed to help stick the post it notes up
- Headers for each of the walls "Stop, Start, Continue"

The Process:

- Every staff member is invited to write down which team processes and behaviors they believe should "Stop, Start or Continue"
- Give the group 30-45 mins to write down their thoughts
- Stick the Post it notes up under the relevant header
- Once the brainstorming is complete, the group will break for 15 minutes
- The facilitator and designated team members will commence grouping items into themes or logical groups
- When the group returns from their break the facilitator will go through the key themes
- All themes and actions will then be recorded, and the team will vote on the validity of each theme.

For items that should stop if there is consensus then these items will stop.

For items that should stay there needs to be consensus and these items will stay.

For new items the group will vote on the priority of the items and individuals or groups will be assigned tasks to develop and initiate the new items.

Regular updates will be required to ensure that new items are actioned in a timely manner.

The Rules:

This is a no holds barred process. Everyone needs to be open and honest with their feedback otherwise you will not get buy in.

No bad language and nothing personal about individuals, this is about the process.

The outcomes of this session will become the new ways of working in the team. It is important to note that this process is useful on an annual basis, irrespective if you have staff turnover or not. Processes can always be improved and this is a perfect way of ensuring that you have continual team buy in.

Norming[15]

Having developed and workshopped both your team's vision and the To-Be processes, you have dealt with "what" needs to be done in the To-Be organisation. Now it is time to address the "how". I have successfully used a "Pillars and Guiding Principles" framework to facilitate this activity—but there are many alternate models and terminology available in management texts and management consultants' kit bags. At its core it is about the values and capabilities your team needs to effectively do the work of the To-Be organisation.

Example:

Here is an example of what the framework for one of my teams looked like. The pillars along the top are what we hope our customers experience when working with us.

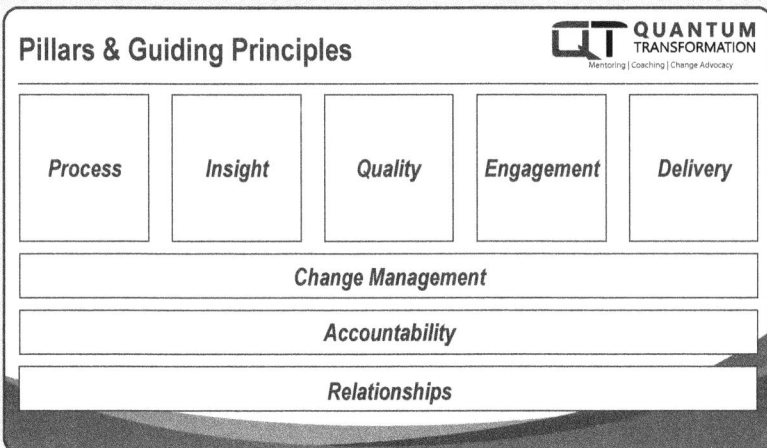

Having determined the pillars, I work with the team to explain and document the detail that constitutes each:

Pillar Detail

QUANTUM TRANSFORMATION
Mentoring | Coaching | Change Advocacy

Process
- Improved adherence to process
- Localisation where applicable to achieve better quality
- Everyone knows what to do and how to do it
- No variances, No excuses

Insight
- Visibility of deliverables
- Visibility of staff utilisation
- Stakeholders are getting what they want when they want it
- Stakeholders don't have to ask they just know

Quality
- Business are assured of quality
- Environments are fit for purpose
- Environments are available rapidly to support delivery
- Test execution is not single point sensitive
- Testing is our last line of defence

Engagement
- Business engagement provides advocacy in the business and business advocacy with us
- Business engagement manages demand
- Business engagement understands and manages expectations

Delivery
- Concurrent projects run effectively to deliver greater throughput
- Project teams working across logical streams to deliver more
- All changes managed and effectively communicated to business stakeholders

📝 Example:

The guiding principles are those competencies and attitudes that should exist within the team to facilitate how we choose to work.

Underpinning Principles Details

QUANTUM TRANSFORMATION
Mentoring | Coaching | Change Advocacy

Change Management:
- Communicate to all affected by the changes we are delivering
- Engage all stakeholders and ensure that the change sticks

Accountability:
- Be responsible for what we deliver and how we deliver

Relationships:
- Forge strong relationships to build a stronger cohesive team
- Look at how we communicate and do this respectfully

It can be useful to translate these principles into behaviours expected of individuals.

Pathway to Success

QUANTUM TRANSFORMATION
Mentoring | Coaching | Change Advocacy

List the ways in which you will succeed in achieving the team vision

For example:
- *Project Management Office are required to enforce the PMM (project management methodology)*
- *Quality Assurance are required to take an active part in post implementation reviews to improve upon process*
- *We are all accountable and need to learn from what went well and what did not go well*
- *No more blame game, we are in this together, we need to have each others backs*

Example:

The final piece in developing "how" the work will get one is to make the future state organisation structure clear. A simple org structure diagram along with any supporting information is all that is required.

Structured to Succeed Detail

QUANTUM TRANSFORMATION
Mentoring | Coaching | Change Advocacy

- *Document how this structure will support success*

  - Project Managers and Analysts will work collaboratively on intersecting processes to develop the best approach
  - All Project Managers will be equipped to deliver their projects within the Project Management Methodology
  - Each Project Manager will be required to adhere strictly to the processes and this will be driven by the Program Manager
  - All Project Managers will need to be certified

  - All Analysts will report into the Senior Analyst
  - All Analysts are equipped to be enabled to achieve the vision with relevant training
  - The vision will be achieved by adherence to processes
  - All Analysts will be certified

Performing[16]

It is during the performing stage that all your team development work gets put into action. Now is the time to encourage your team to think of themselves as a 'problem-solving instrument' where energy is channelled away from planning and into task[17].

In addition to new job/position descriptions and the capability matrix, two other valuable outputs can be generated at this stage—a training plan and career maps. If you have a dedicated Learning and Development Department or a Human Resources Department that has L&D as part of its scope, they may be able to assist in putting these together. Else, as a leader, you and your team members should develop these together. Here are some templates I have found useful.

With any change it is important to provide your team with a map of their career future. This will improve overall performance and motivation. As a leader, career maps will enable you to have constructive conversations with team members about where you see them in the new structure and how they can best add value to the organisation over the immediate and longer term.

One important purpose of these documents is to provide you and your team with a basis for planning and implementing Training and Development and Career Development programs. Do not allow training plans and career maps to stop at the planning and documentation stage. Moving to actual program design, development and implementation will not only demonstrate a commitment from the organisation to improve skills in relation to initial roles in the future organisation, but also to identify and close skill gaps as they apply to other future roles that may be of interest.

Embedding performance metrics

An important step in building your new team is to put performance measures in place. You must be able to demonstrate team and individual performance and performance improvement in the future state organisation.

The best measures are S.M.A.R.T measures[18]. These measures are known for the following attributes:

- *Specific* – target a specific area for improvement[19].
- *Measurable* – quantify or at least suggest an indicator of progress[20].
- *Assignable* – specify who will do it[21].
- *Realistic* – state what results can realistically be achieved, given available resources[22].
- *Time-related* – specify when the result(s) can be achieved[23].

QUANTUM TRANSFORMATION
Mentoring | Coaching | Change Advocacy

TRAINING PLAN

Employee Name: Enter Employee Name Here

Employee Role: Function Manager

Available Courses	0-6 months	6-12 months	12-18 months	18-36 months	Additional Learning	Expected	Booked	Date Booked	Completed	Date Completed	Comments
1.0 Induction											
1.1 Induction (new starter)						X	02/12/2019	Y		2/2/2018	
1.2 Manager Induction								Y		2/2/2018	
2.0 Communication & People/Relationship Management Skills											
2.1 Business Communications		X						N			
2.2 Customer Service		X						N			
2.3 Influencing and Negotiating		X						N			
2.4 Innovation and Creativity				X				N			
2.5 Presentation Skills	X							N			
3.0 Occupational Health & Safety, & Workers' Compensation Skills											
3.1 Provide First Aid (2 days)				X				N			
3.2 Provide First Aid Refresher (1 day)				X				N			
3.3 Emergency Evacuation		X									
3.4 5 Day OHS Managers, Supervisors & OHS Representatives				X				N			
3.5 OHS Refresher Course (for OHS Representatives)				X				N			

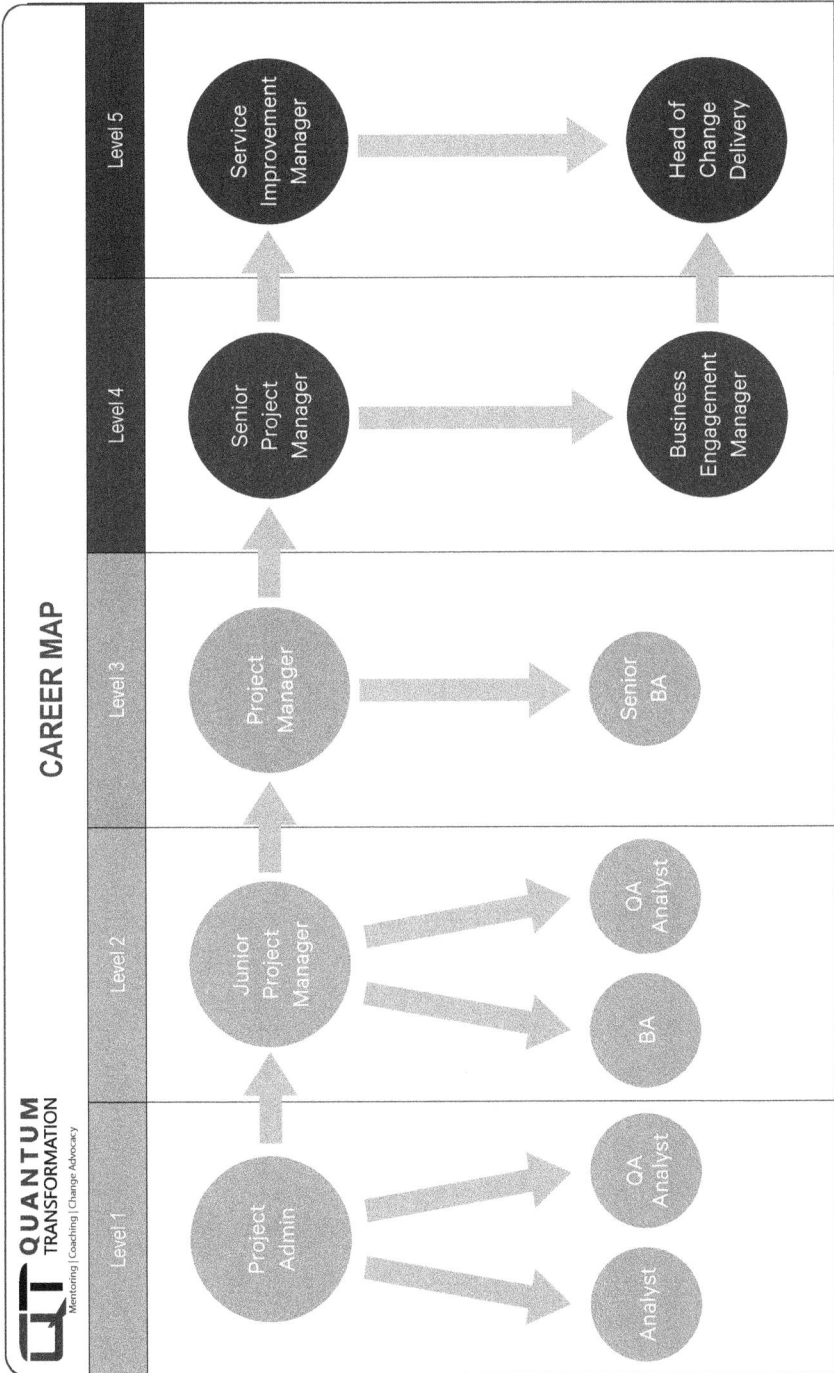

QUANTUM TRANSFORMATION
Mentoring | Coaching | Change Advocacy

CAREER MAP

Level 1 — Project Admin → Analyst, QA Analyst
Level 2 — Junior Project Manager → BA, QA Analyst
Level 3 — Project Manager → Senior BA
Level 4 — Senior Project Manager → Business Engagement Manager
Level 5 — Service Improvement Manager → Head of Change Delivery

📝 Example:

This is an example of the performance metrics I have embedded into a delivery team:

Measures of Success QUANTUM TRANSFORMATION
Mentoring | Coaching | Change Advocacy

- *Document measures of success using SMART measures:*
  - **S**pecific: Well defined, clear, and unambiguous
  - **M**easurable: With specific criteria that measure your progress towards the accomplishment of the goal
  - **A**chievable: Attainable and not impossible to achieve
  - **R**ealistic: Within reach, realistic, and relevant to your life purpose
  - **T**imely: With a clearly defined timeline, including a starting date and a target date. The purpose is to create urgency.

Measures of Success QUANTUM TRANSFORMATION
Mentoring | Coaching | Change Advocacy

Process	95% compliance with Project Management Methodology
	10% tolerance of project budget
Insight	100% Project issues and risks adhere to project methodology tolerances
	100% Self service project reports updated on monthly cycle
Quality	10 recorded environment defects per project
	Time taken to execute is within 5% of forecast
	> 95% deployments successfully tested
Engagement	Team utilisation between 70-80% overall time allocation
	100% Stakeholder meetings held at quarterly intervals
Delivery	>90% projects delivered on time and on budget
	100% projects have an approved business case with agreed ROI

Whenever you put measures in place be sure that they follow the SMART principle[24]. Remember that change is the process of continually renewing the organisation's direction, structure, or capabilities. Without baseline performance metrics it will be impossible to gauge the success of the change or the quality of performance in the new roles.

With any change, ensure that the outcomes you are expecting your team to deliver are achievable. Nothing is more disempowering to individuals and teams than objectives that cannot be met. This does not mean that you cannot have reach targets but making sure that the objectives are fair and reasonable is important.

Change work responsibilities

As you will have gathered from this chapter, change requires a lot of work. As a leader you will not, in fact should not, do it all yourself. A RACI[25] (responsibility assignment matrix) will help you and your team understand who is responsible for which change activities.

Network

The purpose of networking during change is to highlight the value you and your team bring to the change and the future state organisation. This means networking with others involved in the change program. Know who to talk to about what and create a stakeholder engagement plan. There are many templates available, use one that makes sense to you. Here is a template that has worked for me.

QUANTUM
TRANSFORMATION
Mentoring | Coaching | Change Advocacy

RACI (RESPONSIBLE, ACCOUNTABLE, CONSULTED, INFORMED)

PEOPLE/TEAM

Deliverable	Change Champion	Team Lead	Team Member	Manager	Senior Manager	Comments
Team analysis	R	A	I	A	C	
Team restructure	R	A	I	A	C	
Team training	R		I	A		
Ways of working		R	R	A		

A note on Information Technology system changes:

Where IT systems change, you will need to ensure that the business processes and systems align:

Review process flows and ensure that they are granular enough to ensure adherence to the new process. You want to ensure that team members are not reverting to old ways of working or working "off system" (not using the IT system and using work arounds) which will impact productivity and accuracy.

Audit processes to ensure adherence to the process in the first instance until the system is fully embedded and being used as intended. Document possible tips and tricks to use the system for example: FAQ's (frequently asked questions). Any tools that ensure that the IT system is embedded into your team will assist in improving use and productivity in the future.

Provide feedback to the IT function with possible improvements as you continue to work with the system. Note however that change requests may not align with the systems feature set and other departments and may not be delivered. There will be budgetary constraints on the IT function and the business so ensure that you are transparent with your team about the possibility that they may not get all the functionality they want immediately. Sometimes you will have to work with what is approved.

QUANTUM TRANSFORMATION
Mentoring | Coaching | Change Advocacy

STAKEHOLDER ENGAGEMENT PLAN

	Key Stakeholder (Individual/Group)	What role will they play in the change activity?	How will you engage them?	When will you follow up?	How will you know you've gained their commitment?
1	CEO	Will be creating the vision for the change and articulating this. Key decision maker.	Via written communication, town hall meetings and avenues advised by the change team	During open forums as advised by the change team	Via line manager communications
2	Line Manager	Will be explaining the vision and accountable for ensuring continued delivery	Direct communications (verbally and written)	Set up regular face to face sessions	Received in writing where possible. If verbal then followed up in writing
3	Team Leads	Will be assisting with the implementation of the change activities. Ensure that team are continuing to deliver during the change	Direct communications (verbally and written)	Set up regular face to face sessions. Regular group planning sessions	Verbal and written feedback on a regular basis
4					
5					
6					
7					
8					
9					
10					

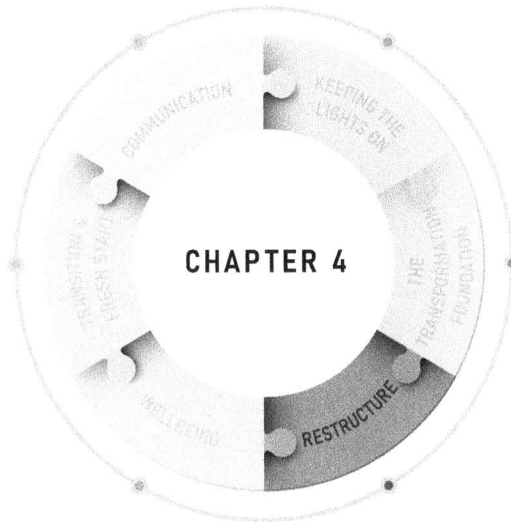

CHAPTER 4

The Restructure Piece

It is almost certain that transitioning to the To-Be state of the organisation will result in a restructure of the organisation and your team. A restructure may mean losing or gaining team members. There may be team members who use this as an opportunity to re-evaluate their role within the organisation and choose to leave. Others may remain but be affected by survivors' guilt which could increase anxiety.[1] In this chapter I focus on the very difficult task of letting people go—there is nowhere in the transition from As-Is to To-Be where your leadership will be more needed.

The three R's – reduction, retrenchment and redundancy

Reduction, retrenchment and redundancy occur when outputs you have been delivering to your organisation are outsourced, automated or no longer required. In extreme cases whole functions may be shut down. In other cases, there may be a reduction in team size.

When you have a view on what will stop, you will need to look at your teams' structure and capabilities and make decisions, typically in conjunction with senior leadership, about team reduction, retrenchments or redundancies.

Whatever the decision you need to encourage knowledge transfer and allow your team the time to do this as part of their day to day tasks. Creating knowledge bases and cross training team members will remove single point sensitivity and should the need to downsize become apparent you will be better prepared. This is an important action to ensure that when team members leave you retain your ability to continue to service your organisation.

Reduction

Focus on who you need so that the most important and immediate work required to keep your business operating gets done. If the reduction is a temporary one you may have the option of standing team members down and reemploying them later. If it is a more permanent reduction it is essential that you work through what needs to be delivered and retain the skills required. For those retained, typically they are asked to take on more work and responsibility. Facilitating a handover is important for those left holding the fort.

Look at the work that will add the most value to the organisation. Look at multifaceted team members, those who can work in more than one role. By focusing on team members who can be mobilised to many different areas you will be able to produce more for the business. Although this is a challenging time it is also a time of opportunity. Use this time as a way of building your "perfect" team. Remove any emotion from your decision making and focus on what you will be expected to achieve. The To-Be business process maps are critical at this point. When you make decisions in this way it will make the inevitable conversations easier, as your rationale will be sound and based on what is best for the business.

It is important to think about who you will keep and who you will let go as early as possible. When the decision is made to reduce you will want to be on the front foot. Unfortunately, this is going to be one of the times when you will not be able to share the planning with your team. You are going to need your team's continued focus until the decision to downsize is made.

At this time, as a leader, you may feel very isolated. You are making decisions about peoples' livelihood. This is a burden that you will have to carry. You also need to focus on your own well-being, so that you can continue to deliver what the business needs and so those who remain can continue to deliver.

In certain circumstances it is possible that staff members being stood down may seek governmental assistance. For those in countries that do not have social services to fall back on, the decision of who to let go and who to keep will be even more challenging. Make sure you work with your Human Resources team to ensure those stood down or let go receive whatever support they are entitled to.

Redundancies and retrenchment

The difference between redundancy and retrenchment is subtle but needs to be understood.

- A redundancy occurs when a specific position in a business is no longer required[2]
- A retrenchment occurs when an employee loses their position and cannot be redeployed because no other suitable position exists[3]

Irrespective of whether a role is made redundant or an employee is retrenched the key thing to remember is that you may not be able to replace the role within the business when the business returns to a steady state. Therefore, make sure that the roles or people you remove are not going to be needed in the medium or long term.

Depending on your jurisdiction's employment law, there may be differing time frames within which you can't replace or back fill a role that has been made redundant or an individual who has been retrenched. Be sure to discuss these options with your Human Resources department to ensure you are well informed.

Depending on the position you hold within your organisation, decisions on redundancies or retrenchments may not be yours. If you find yourself in the situation where decisions that impact your team are being made and you are not being consulted—speak up! Ensure that you have rational arguments documented and at the ready should you be required to justify keeping specific team members.

For some organisations, an expediate way of making decisions is to look at "last on, first off". This approach rarely results in the best decisions, because recent hires are often those with skills your team has specifically needed. Again, if you believe the approach being taken will negatively impact your ability to deliver in the short/ medium term, be prepared to stand up and argue your case.

During the time you are working through these difficult issues, it is possible that team members may worry their role may be at risk. If this is the case, you may start to see atypical behaviours from team members such as:

- Aggression towards each other
- Closed interactions
- Lack of sharing knowledge even when repeatedly requested
- Silos re-emerging after they had previously been broken down

This not unusual as fear takes over. When individuals feel that their livelihood is at risk, they may behave counterintuitively. However, there may be others who will step up to help with getting the job done. They will assist others and make sure that everything they are working on is in a state to be easily handed over.

Irrespective of how team members behave you will need to ensure that you have a solid handover plan in place. This may be difficult as you may not be able to speak to your team about the reasons for handovers. You will need to revert to your communications plan. Focus on what you are at liberty to say and on providing meaningful work for your team to continue with. Useful and meaningful work at this time might simply be asking each team member to document what they do on a daily basis. Whatever you decide, keep people busy with meaningful work until it is time to reduce the team size.

It is also important to add, that a lot of what your team is working on may fall to you. So, ensure that you are well across the detail of their roles, as it may be expected that you keep the lights on with a much smaller team.

Delivering the message

There is a lot of literature on how best to deliver a redundancy or retrenchment message to team members. Remember this is an organisational change situation, NOT performance management separation, which has quite a different approach. In a performance management situation, your Human Resources team will have performance management frameworks you will need to use.

Generally, you will want to deliver the message face to face, but you may also need to consider how you best do it if working remotely is a consideration.

This is the general process I follow. I have made some notations to reflect the nuances of remote conversations.

1. Prepare yourself. Have all your documentation ready.
2. Book a private room to have the discussion in. (A room with technology will be required for remote conversations)

3. Have tissues ready, just in case. (Allow the person time to get tissues if necessary, in remote discussions)

4. Step straight into the conversation. This is going to be tough enough for both parties so jump directly into the conversation. If you feel yourself getting emotional during the conversation, it is ok to take a breath and perhaps say "I have some difficult news to share, and this is a hard conversation for me to have".

5. Have an introduction prepared. Your Human Resources department may provide a script for you to follow. ie: The business is under great stress and decisions have been made regarding your position.

6. Advise that this was a difficult decision and highlight some of the team member's strengths and positive contributions.

7. Explain why this is happening to this individual but remember it is the role that is going. It is not about performance.

8. Explain why this is happening now.

9. Explain the package being provided.

10. Express your gratitude for the good work done.

11. No matter how well the conversation goes, individuals will respond differently or unexpectedly. You will need to make it clear that any equipment the individual has is company owned and will need to be returned. Provide final details e.g.: returning of pass codes, keys, credit cards, equipment. (If you are working remotely ensure you have plans to collect company equipment.) Ensure the IT department has arranged for all access to be revoked to coincide with the end of your conversation.

12. Escort the individual out or terminate the remote meeting.

13. Follow required IT processes for access to network, systems etc.

14. Immediately have a meeting with your team to explain what has happened. They will be impacted by this change and will need time to process this.

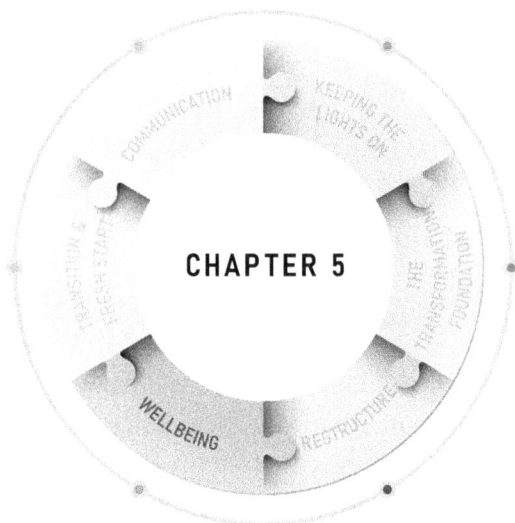

CHAPTER 5

The Wellbeing Piece

🖐 Wellbeing starts with us as leaders

We cannot nurture our team's wellbeing if we are not feeling secure and calm ourselves. Practice reflection—a reflective leader is a grounded leader. Reflect on your own value to the organisation and your team. Focus on your strength and resilience. Be satisfied with small steps, large change is a marathon and not a sprint[1]. Remain positive.

As leaders we want to inspire our teams to consistently deliver high quality work. We want our teams to understand the value they bring and encourage them to challenge the status quo and bring energy to their role[2]. We cannot expect them to be able to do this if they do not feel safe and cared for. This is true whether your team is being impacted by a change or not. In this chapter we explore a number of concepts and initiatives you can focus on to help with team wellbeing.

A shared direction

An important part of maintaining wellbeing is to ensure your team feels like they belong with the rest of the organisation. Feeling they are the "odd department out" will undermine this sense of belonging. To achieve this, ensure that your team deeply understands the organisation's vision and overall strategy. You have likely discussed this with your team regularly over time.

If you have done a good job at engaging your team with the organisation's strategy, and they have signed up to it—what happens to their commitment when change tosses an embedded strategy out the window and teams are asked to sign up to a new one? This is a major pain point in the organisation's change journey. Maintaining their and your sense of equilibrium and wellbeing may be quite difficult at this point—job satisfaction may decline. This decline may impact your team's productivity and your ability to continue to deliver. An overall lethargy may overcome your team. People may take short cuts, leave tasks unfinished, need to take personal time off work.

You must start again with the new vision and strategy. Distribute it in written form, discuss it and debate it regularly with your team. Stress how your team's vision, pillars and guiding principles are an important enabling force in achieving it.

Team resilience

It is well understood that change is a major stressor in organisational life. Why do individuals struggle so much with change? The answer is complicated but at its core it stems from an individual's sense of self. If the change potentially impacts our sense of who we are, it will activate powerful motivations to return to the status quo[3].

When leading through a transformation, you need to recognise if your team is experiencing these emotions and assess their ability to recover and adapt quickly—this ability is described as resilience. If the organisation has had multiple failed change efforts your team's resilience may be low, when confronted with another change program. To build resilience, get your team members actively involved in the change. Enabling them to take control of elements of the change will give them ownership and return some control over their working world[4].

📝 Example:

On one occasion I was particularly keen to get my team involved in change work as they were feeling disengaged. I discussed this with the change champions. We agreed to get my team working side by side with them mapping the As-Is state to the To-Be state. The team worked with each department on implementing the new ways of working to ensure greater adoption across the business. One aspect of this project was to identify value-added activities that could be sold to customers.

My team was required to monitor the changes and ensure that the revenue delivered from the value-added projects was tracked and reported upon. This work was highly valued by the organisation's leadership and ensured that my team was recognised and engaged throughout the course of the change.

Build culture

A positive workplace culture and team wellbeing go hand in hand. Your team has its own culture. If the culture is strong, it will help weather the change storm. When the culture is poor, leading through a change is much harder. One way to assist in gaining traction with the changes and maintaining team wellbeing is to leverage the strong parts of your current culture. Even if the broader organisation does not have a strong, positive culture—you can still work on the culture at your team level.

Over time I have built strong cultures in my teams by encouraging my people to challenge the status quo. When they do suggest something that needs to change, I challenge them to own the change and make it better. They are empowered and supported, and I constantly tell them "*I have your back*".

Develop an advocacy culture

Advocacy is the process of speaking up for others and ensuring that everyone is treated fairly and equitably across your team and the broader organisation. An advocacy culture is a culture where all members of the team feel safe to support each other and challenge the status quo without retribution.

Creating an equitable workplace where respectful challenge is supported will create an advocacy culture. If people within your team feel that they cannot speak up, that they do not have a voice, you must change this. By creating this cultural norm, you provide your team members with an avenue of support from within the team.

We need to become and create advocates within and across the organisation. It can take time to develop a cultural norm such as advocacy. It starts by leaders supporting people at the individual level, then encouraging team members to advocate for others who are feeling pain or attempting to pursue opportunities. The culture will then grow across teams, departments and the organisation and will break down silos down and develop organisation wide respect.

Example:

I recently came across a junior employee who was desperate to prove his worth within the organisation. His manager told me that she believed the junior wanted the opportunity to work on a highly sought-after project. She felt that it would be a great way of enabling him to learn and grow and get some exposure to the rest of the organisation.

The manager was adamant that this was a good move for the business and the employee, and she advocated strongly for the opportunity. I agreed based on the passion and advocacy of the manager.

The junior delivered the project successfully and has now received a well-deserved promotion. Had we not had an advocacy culture in the team then this may not have taken place and we may have lost a talented team member.

————— ••• —————

If you are unsure about your culture, ask yourself: Have you built a psychologically safe work environment[5]? This is an environment where your team members feel empowered to challenge the status quo, to be able to have open and honest conversations with colleagues, to always be looking at ways of improving the way the team functions. If you have answered yes to these, then you have built a strong positive culture.

If you have not, then there is more work to be done. Start this work by:

- Evaluating your on-boarding process. Does it provide new starters with all the information to easily start with the business?
- Observing interactions across the team. Do your team members speak respectfully to each other? Is there open and honest communication? Does the team innovate together and support each other?
- Gauging staff retention. If your staff retention is low, it is a good sign that team members enjoy the working

environment and you have a strong culture. If is it high, direct your efforts at bolstering the team environment.

- Speaking regularly and honestly with team members to understand their perception of the team culture. Ask what can be improved and look at ways of implementing their ideas.

Building culture from adversity

The recent COVID-19 response has placed teams and organisations in an unlikely position of having a majority of team members working remotely and not in offices. A global response to a pandemic has created a bond between team members. When the circumstances revert back to the way they were before the crisis, their shared stories of overcoming the hardships will become a part of the DNA of the team and organisation.

Just as it was during other world events (such as The Great Depression, WWI, WWII and the GFC) so it will be with COVID-19. This will become a bonding experience between people in your organisation. Building cultural main stays in your team is about having shared experiences.

When your team goes through a traumatic event, there is a sense of survival when you come out the other side.

Support your team

Change can be daunting, particularly when there is the possibility that it could affect one's livelihood. Therefore, it is extremely important that your team feels they have your support. Here are some pragmatic ways you can demonstrate your support as the change kicks in.

1. Ensure your team has a forum to be heard. Discussing the change with each other will build a stronger bond across the team. Encourage sharing of experiences and stories. Tell your team how much you appreciate them. Show them by involving them, communicating with them, and listening to them. Get them access to the change champions if they want to talk to them directly.

    > Regular team meetings are invaluable; however, forums should include one on one meetings as well so that team members can speak with you directly. Some team members may not be comfortable raising concerns in an open forum. During any change set up multiple avenues of communication.

2. Ensure your team knows what you expect of them, and that their outputs are valuable to you and the organisation. Display confidence in their ability to achieve what is required. Be realistic about what you and they can and can't control and communicate this to your team as well. There is no need for them to waste time and energy on things that are outside of their span of control.

    > During change it is especially important that your team are working on meaningful deliverables. Giving people "busy" work will have a disempowering effect on them. They need to know that what they are delivering is needed. I generally focus on work that is currently in flight within my team. I refer to business cases and the value that the work is providing to the organisation.

3. Celebrate small successes along the way—celebrations are strong motivators. Your team will feel recognised and valued. Celebrations do not have to be large and may be budgetarily constrained. Sometimes a simple written or verbal thank you from you can go a long way.

    > Here are some examples of the things I do to recognise the hard work of my team during times of change:

- Have call outs of individuals and their achievements during team meetings.
- Rewards and recognition across the department with small gifts such as chocolates, movie vouchers (cognizant of budgetary constraints).
- In organisations that have weekly or monthly newsletters I provide call outs for team members or groups that have delivered value.
- Team lunches or morning teas to celebrate key project milestones.

4. Look for change advocates and engage them to help the team feel supported. A change advocate will be a team member who embraces change and adds a level of positivity to the team dynamic. These individuals will have a high tolerance for ambiguity and a low level of cynicism towards change[6].

> Your change advocates may change depending on the nature of the situation. You may have someone in your team who you think would be the perfect change advocate but when the change commences, they become defensive and conflicted. Depending on "what's in it for them" you may need different advocates for different changes.

5. Ensure that your team are involved in the change efforts where possible. This involvement will increase the success of the change implementation[7].

> As mentioned in previous chapters working with the change champions is an example of getting involved in the change. Another way is to have team members head up different projects—let them run with projects that will improve the way you operate post change.

6. Utilise every opportunity to interact with your team. Legitimise the change, encourage challenges and have answers ready for the questions that will come.

> I use my one on one sessions for this. It really allows for honest communications and enables me to reiterate the importance of the changes we are facing.

7. Don't focus too much energy on the negative team members. If your culture is strong and your change advocates are inspiring, then the peer pressure will make its way to the negative team members, eventually.

> Although this may seem harsh, during a change I do not have a lot of time to focus on the negative team members. They have the opportunity to speak with me during the one to one session, but I always maintain my composure and stay on message with them. As the change progresses and more and more of the team are on board with it, the negative team members tend to fall in line with peer pressure.

Employee assistance

Your organisation may have an employee assistance program (EAP) or have mental health first aiders. Their purpose is to reduce the potential of losing team members experiencing severe stress and to provide ongoing independent psychological support if required. When team members are having difficulty with change these programs will become part of your arsenal. If you believe one or more of your team members needs this support and your organisation does not have it in place—speak to your Human Resources team to see what they can arrange.

Mindfulness

Mindfulness is valuable for both leaders and team members. It is a great way to help employees relieve stress and bring back some balance and calm. It helps people to focus on the day-to-day work and to improve productivity during change. If you are a mindfulness practitioner, you may be able to train your staff in these techniques. If you are not, then it might be a good time to bring in professionals to assist you. A simple Google search will provide resources and organisations that you can tap into to assist with mindfulness training.

Practice mindfulness—a mindful leader is a calm leader

Change is stressful. This is natural response when things are out of your control. As hard as it may be, it is extremely important to remain calm and positive. Your emotional state will impact on your ability to do this. Practicing mindfulness can help.

So, what is mindfulness? "Mindfulness is the psychological process of purposely bringing one's attention to experiences occurring in the present moment without judgment, which one can develop through the practice of meditation and through other training" Wikipedia (5/11/2019)[8]

Simply put, mindfulness is about thinking about the present moment, not focussing on the "what ifs" and the things that happened in the past[9].

We have all gone through change in the past and it is natural to recall those experiences, whether negative or positive, and allow them to influence the way we approach the current change. The problem with this is that the situations, and teams will be very different. If you lead the same way as you did in past change projects, you may find yourself not open to current information and you may act ineffectively.

Leading mindfully means actively listening to your team. You do not interpret or judge what they are saying through your past lens, you listen with fresh ears. You update your plans on basis of the feedback you are receiving.

"Being mindful means that we suspend judgement for a time, set aside our immediate goals for the future, and take in the present moment as it is rather than as we would like it to be." Mark Williams"[10]

Encourage movement/exercise

When your team is feeling overwhelmed by the changes ahead of them, it is good to find ways to get them moving. Exercise enables individuals to remove themselves from a stressful situation and to rethink options. Look for ways of adding movement to the day to day activities in your team. This doesn't mean paying for everyone to join a gym.

Here are some options you may want to consider:

- Individual meetings can be walking meetings (weather permitting)
- Set up weekly walking sessions with the team and encourage involvement
- Bring in yoga instructors and set up weekly yoga/stretching sessions
- Encourage standing desks or fit balls instead of chairs
- Keep a steps tally and gamify the team's steps per day

Take a walk together

There have been many times during major transformations that I have had to guide emotional team members through changes. When individuals become emotional and need to express their feelings it can be uncomfortable for them to do so in an office environment. It may make others in the office uncomfortable as well.

Suggesting a walk outside will have a two-fold effect. Firstly, it will remove the individual from the environment which is causing the distress. Secondly it will get them moving. When people start moving, they become more focussed on the activity than on the cause of their distress. Once the individual is calm it is easier to have a conversation where you can actively listen to their concerns and alleviate them.

Gratitude practice[11]

Gratitude practice is about being grateful for what you have and focussing on the positives in the workplace[12]. Moving from a place of fear to a place of calm. Gratitude practice is the process of recognising the good in our lives and workplaces and focussing on it. It enables us to reframe things we perceive as negative and to see the good in a situation.

Gratitude practice facilitates a reduction in stress caused by the organisational change your team is experiencing. By focussing on the good that surrounds them your team may start to reframe the change and see the positive outcomes that may come from it.

Here are some ways of implementing gratitude practice which you can suggest to your team:

- Keeping a journal of things you are grateful for (*e.g. "I am grateful that IT was able to fix the network so quickly"*)[13]

- Making some time during the day to express gratitude to others for things they are and have done (e.g. *"Thank you for taking time to explain the policy to our new team member, I am very grateful"*)[14]
- When something good is experienced share this with colleagues (e.g. *"I had such a good meeting with the CEO, she is so happy with how we are coping with the new systems"*)
- Appreciate nature. When you're taking your walking meeting, take time to appreciate nature.[15]
- Simply think positive thoughts[16]

You may wish to research other options that you can introduce to your team. Some team members may embrace this, and others may not—do not force it. Embracing gratitude is a choice.

One thing that I like to do on a daily basis as I make my way to work in the morning is to think about those things in my life that I am grateful for.

I find that as I think about my family, my friends and my colleagues I have a sense of peace. I feel gratitude for those individuals in my world who have helped me, challenged me and supported me and this grounds me and prepares me for my day.

When I am working through my greatest challenges, this practice brings me back to what is truly important and enables me to think clearly each day and welcome what may come.

Get involved in social responsibility[17]

In addition to gratitude practice you may want to suggest that your team get involved in social responsibility programs. If your organisation offers these then promote involvement within your team.

If gratitude practice helps individuals see the bigger picture—what better way of seeing it in action than getting involved in a program that gives something back to the community. This will help your team focus on the bigger picture and provide a sense of purpose and contribution.

If your organisation does not have social responsibility programs, then there is no better time to undertake some research into programs that you can suggest. Just as with gratitude practice you can encourage but do not force team members to get involved. Let them choose the things that resonate with them.

I have worked with organisations that do not have many avenues for social responsibility activities. Here are some of the things that I have suggested to them:

- Set up fund raisers within the office for various organisations. These have included bake sales where we bake and sell our items to the team for morning/afternoon tea.
- Volunteering time to a local soup kitchen – e.g. Salvation Army.
- Volunteering time to environmental organisations – planting trees around your major capital cities.

Many organisations have information on their websites explaining how other organisations can support them. Personally, I dedicate my time to non-profit organisations that resonate with me. You may not think that the skills you have may be of use but simply asking "what can I do to help" will give any non-profit organisation the ability to advise what they need. From here you can decide how best you can help. Giving something back to your local community really helps when other things are out of your control.

Emotional intelligence training

Emotional intelligence training[18] is the process of improving each team member's EQ (emotional quotient). It is about exploring the individual's self-perception and acknowledging that the organisational change may be impacting them more than they realise.

For this sort of training I recommend that you invest in bringing a registered practitioner in EQ training. They will be able to develop a structured training session that you and your team members can attend. A Google search will provide you with local training organisations that will be able to tailor training to suit your needs.

The key areas that you want to ensure are covered in this training are:

- Self-perception
- Self-expression
- Interpersonal skills
- Decision making
- Stress management

These skills will assist your team members to understand themselves and help them to connect with other team members in a constructive way. By having a clear understanding of how they are dealing with the organisational change, your team members will become more empathetic with others. This in turn will help relieve stress and bring a greater level of connectedness across your team.

Additional ideas to maintain well-being

There are other ways to improve wellbeing within your team. These include:

- flexible working arrangements[19]
- mentoring and coaching

- team building activities
- reward and recognition

The idea is to bring a sense of fulfillment and joy back into the workplace whilst you are undergoing change. The list is endless, and these are just some ideas that I believe may help your team members to reconnect with each other during the changes ahead. Your organisation may have some or all these programs in place. If they do, then I urge you to take advantage of as many of them as you can. Where they do not, then you may need to talk to your Human Resources department to see if they can help you implement some of them.

———— ••• ————

Despite your efforts, there may be people in your team who are negative and cynical throughout the change. This is not a failure on your part, it is indicative of someone with a low tolerance for ambiguity[20]. Change is by nature ambiguous—and for periods of time at least, there is nothing you can do about it. Individuals who fall into this category may choose to leave the organisation or may be mobilised elsewhere. This is sometimes the by-product of change, and it is best to accept it. Focus your work on the core group of your team who are positive about the future.

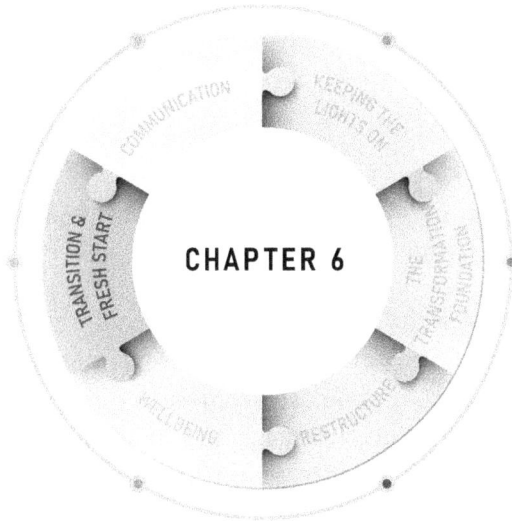

CHAPTER 6

The Transition and Fresh Start Piece

It is important to get to a steady state as quickly as possible. With any change there are things that need to be taken care of once the change team has disbanded and the change has been implemented.

Sometimes it is only when the transition to the future organisation is complete that the devastation the fear of change has caused becomes clear. As already touched on in previous chapters, this fear will have come from a perceived/real loss of control[1]. If team members continue to feel a loss of control after transitioning to the new organisation, it can lead to intense protectionist behaviour which may manifest in several ways:

1. Individual team members will protect their knowledge and cease sharing information with and across teams
2. Silos will begin to form or strengthen
3. Any perceived/actual risks will be avoided
4. Courageous/innovative acts will be discouraged

5. Actions that shine a light on individuals or the team will be avoided

These behaviours may not sit well with senior leadership who are looking for a high functioning new organisation.

To counter the scarcity mindset[2] the use of mindfulness, gratitude practice and emotional intelligence training is a great place to start. Ensure that the language you use promotes a mindset of abundance. The aim is to use positive language and focus on the wins and the opportunities. Together with your team, look for resolutions to problems and get working on the solutions.

Leading a team that is becoming increasingly myopic requires you to acknowledge the fear that is present. Don't trivialise the emotional impact that the change has had on your team. Embrace it and re-focus on the vision of the new organisation.

Breaking down silos

As your team emerges from change into the new organisation, they will discover that the rest of the organisation has changed around them. It is natural to gravitate inward to the known work of one's own team. Instead of allowing your team to become myopic in its vision look for ways in which your team can broaden its reach, build and strengthen relationships across the organisation with a view to breaking down silos.

Depending on the nature of the change you may find it has impacted other teams more than yours. Even if this is not the case it is still important for you and your team to understand the change that others are dealing with. Eventually the change will cascade across the organisation and impact all teams to a varying degree. If you think of your organisation as an organism, any change to one part of the organism will impact the whole.

If your team works empathetically with other teams—you will be well on the way to building solid relationships across the new organisation. This will improve the chances of the change sticking and improve cohesion across departments[3].

Example:

I commenced a role where the previous incumbent had negatively impacted the way in which the team interacted with other teams in the department. In fact, it was so bad that the teams did not speak to each other at all. There were stories of yelling matches across the department, team meetings that got so out of control that team members would walk out of the meeting in tears.

There was a culture of blame between the teams and this was impacting the entire department's ability to deliver successful projects to the business.

I was advised that there were some issues between the teams, but I had no idea how bad the problem was. I could not understand how an entire department could get to this place, where there was such a sense of distrust that it not only impacted delivery but impacted people on a personal level too.

My role was to improve delivery to the business, and I could not do that with such a great divide between teams. The silos seemed insurmountable at the time and I was concerned that this may be something I could not solve.

So, I spent the first month speaking with each team member across the department. I had no history of the underlying issues, so I needed to hear the grievances for myself from everyone involved.

Once I had gathered my information it became clear to me that my team members had no idea of how the work they were doing impacted other team members. They had no idea of the pressures in other teams and no understanding of the complexities that others had to manage every day.

When an issue would arise, the teams would blame each other. Instead of seeing issues as opportunities to improve they used these as weapons against the other teams. I took on a four-pronged approach to break down the silos. This approach was built into each person's performance measures:

1. Walk a Mile – Each team member had to work in another team to understand what the other team members had to contend with on a daily basis.

2. Develop yourself – Each team member would be mentored by their leader with the express purpose of addressing the issues across the team.

3. Learn Something new – Each team member was required to undertake learning something new from the other team. The purpose being to gain an understanding of the challenges others were facing.

4. Reach target – Look at a way of improving a process or function within another team and help them improve their ways of working.

Each person needed to understand the impact they were having on the other teams and look at opportunities to improve it. The outcome was significant as my team began to understand the profound impact they were having on the other teams. Once there was a common understanding the teams began to work well together.

Walk a mile

There is an adage which says you will never understand another person's position until you *"walk a mile in their shoes"*. The same goes for working in an organisation that has undertaken significant change.

To build a greater understanding across teams you need to understand the various ways of working in the new organisation. Each department or team will work in a different new way and the nuances are what will cause friction if not clearly understood. With this understanding it becomes easier for teams to collaborate.

Your team does not work in isolation and by building bridges across the various newly structured teams you will break down barriers which will impact your ability to deliver. By walking a mile in their shoes, you will gain insight into the new challenges they face, and you may find that your challenges are similar.

Share stories

Stories have been used for thousands of years to share tales of gallantry, heroism, survival and defeat. In many cultures they are the very foundation from which people come together. This is no different in an organisation.

When you have worked through similar challenges the stories you tell will bring you together. Story telling highlights the shared experience. It will become the tapestry that binds your team together and will help create new connections with other teams.

You should maintain a positive approach to the story telling, where you can. These stories will become part of your culture. Working towards staving off the cynicism that may have crept in during the change process will help to build a strong culture for the new organisation. You will find that your team will start to put together its own stories, your role as a leader is to help guide the narrative.

Example:

Once when working with a dysfunctional team I had the idea of sharing stories from times of extreme conflict. I had wanted my team and the department to understand that so much more could be achieved if we worked together on a common goal.

At the time I was volunteering for a naval association, working with World War 2 Veterans. I proposed to my manager that we bring in one of the Veterans to speak to the team about their time in the navy during the war. My manager loved this idea, so we brought him in.

We held a team meeting and the Veteran willingly gave his time to speak to our department about living through a world war. He talked about the importance of teamwork, about having each other's back and how to follow procedure because your life depended on it.

He talked about courage under fire and how the friendships were forged amongst the crew. He talked about post war Australia and the challenges that followed. He talked about the joy of speaking with us and how he hoped his stories would help us become a strong team.

After this session there was a marked changed in the department. Little petty squabbles seemed to disappear. Team members worked at improving processes and actively listening to each other.

This small act of sharing helped to bring cohesion to the team and added to our story as a department.

Intentional silos

There are times when an organisation will have intentionally created silos. This will generally happen when there are large projects that need resources ring fenced to deliver. This can create feelings of negativity outside the silo as people see the siloed team getting resources, management attention and praise that they are not.

It will typically be during the transition piece, that the siloed team will need to be integrated back into the organisation and this will require maturity from others. Therefore, it is important to ensure that your team has understood the rationale for the silo and the plan for integration back into business as usual teams.

Example:

I have worked in Information Technology for many years and the intentional silo is used when we have a major program of work that needs to be delivered. The business chooses to set up a team with the sole purpose of delivering that program. Once the delivery is done and the program is transitioned to the support function, the team is disbanded.

I worked in a silo that was set up to deliver an optimisation tool to the transport company that funded the organisation. The entire business unit was set up to develop and deliver a solution across the entire organisation. When the solution was delivered the business, unit was disbanded, and staff were either moved to other business units within the organisation or let go.

Build relationships

Building relationships is a key part of any transition. Ensuring that you have strong respectful relationships within your team will only take you halfway. We have covered breaking down siloe and understanding how the change has impacted other teams— this section looks at ways of building relationships across teams/ departments.

Individual level

- <u>Secondments</u> will enable team members to work within other teams to understand what they are responsible for. This will also provide individuals with training in the work of other departments and will expose them to other potential opportunities.
- <u>Hot desks</u> enable individuals to move within different departments. This encourages conversation, sharing of stories and building a sense of connectedness across teams.

Team level

- Have team members work with other teams on <u>joint projects</u> to build stronger bonds and better outcomes for the organisation.
- If your team is in a support function implementing <u>business partnering</u> forces regular communication with internal client teams. This also provides a mechanism for team members to become known to different departments and to elevate their internal brand.
- Link <u>performance measures</u> to relationship building. If you align some performance metrics around the need to work across teams or get involved (where possible) in partnering or building relationships, then take up will be easier.

Business partnering is the process of building advocacy for one department inside another department. For example, business partnering within the IT function. The purpose of this was to provide IT advocacy within the business and business advocacy within IT.

I had needed to improve the perception of the IT function across the organisation and to do this I needed to have team members work with the business stakeholders to understand the problems that were being faced and how IT could better support them.

I needed business stakeholders to feel listened to. I needed business stakeholders to become advocates for IT. When this was set up, I was able to gain a better understanding of the challenges the business was facing. This in turn enabled me to resource key business projects affectively and deliver greater value to the business.

Onboarding

Onboard any new employees into your team using your To-Be business process maps. This includes individuals who have moved across from other teams or people brought in to back fill if team members have left the organisation.

Most organisations will have a basic induction protocol, but you need to ensure it us updated to reflect the changes to the organisation and particularly any changes to your team. There are some additional things you may find useful when bringing team members into your team in order to build a strong team culture from the outset:

A 3-5-day program which provides the new team member with all your ways of working and processes. If electronic links are available, make sure that they have access to these. If you work remotely make sure that instructions on how to do this are clear.

- Assign a <u>buddy</u> from within the team. Someone in your team who will become the single point of contact in the first few weeks for the new starter. If the person coming into your team is from another department, still assign a buddy. There will be questions that will require answers and your new team member will be feeling a little uncertain. Having someone provide answers quickly will reduce uncertainty so they can hit the ground running.
- Arrange a <u>team lunch</u> if possible. Having an informal team lunch where new starters get to know other members of

the team helps to make people feel welcome and part of something greater than themselves.

- Set up <u>one to one</u> meetings for the first couple of weeks with the new starter. This will reinforce the team culture and the supportive way you lead your team. If they have come from another team this is very important. They may have misgivings following the change and you need to start building trust immediately.

Documents

Once the change is effectively complete you may wish to revisit the documents you created to guide your change journey and decide if you want to adopt them as business as usual. Any that you do should be checked to ensure they align with the vision of the new organisation. For example, even though the change may be considered done, you will still need to continue team communications and may wish to keep your communications plan updated.

Continue your focus on team wins

Continue to focus on wins within the team post change completion. Embedding change is about providing positive anchors[4] from within the new organisation. Use the opportunity to celebrate the wins with a focus on the change achieved.

Example:

I have found it useful to use a visual display unit (score board or VDU) to show how well the team is delivering to the organisation. Having a VDU will allow your team to see how their work is impacting the organisation.

If you have ever worked in an agile environment, then the example below will be very clear to you. This example is of a SCRUM board used to track delivery on a two-weekly basis (in an agile framework this is known as a Sprint).

The purpose of the SCRUM board (or visual display unit) is to show progress undertaken on a daily basis. This can be easily adapted by teams to display at project, program or at task level. An electronic SCRUM board can also be adopted as long as everyone in the team has access to it.

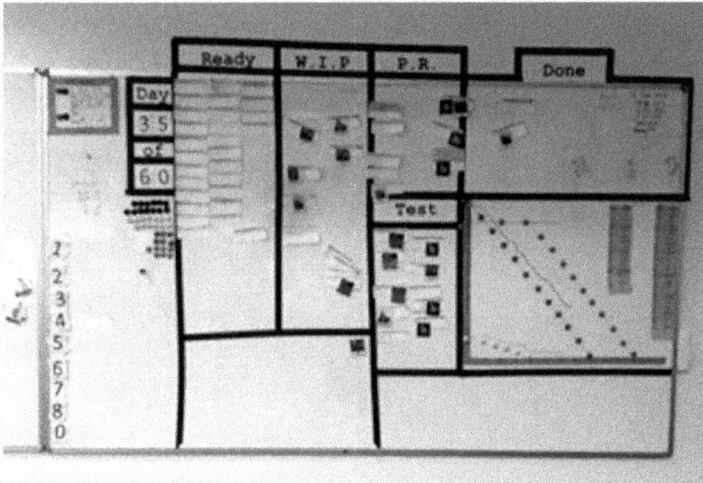

Meet new leadership

If the change has impacted senior stakeholders, you will need to introduce yourself and your team to the new leadership. You want new leaders to know what you and your team have done to support the organisation through the change and how you continued to deliver value during the journey. Demonstrate that you have adopted the new ways of working and have hit the ground running. Have your elevator pitch prepared in order to be ready at any time.

Test that your goals and key performance metrics are aligned with those of the new leaders. This will ensure that you are clear on what is expected of you and of your team and how you best align with the new organisation's goals.

📝 **Example of a delivery department elevator pitch:**

"My department focusses on project delivery of IT software applications, IT infrastructure and eCommerce applications that support our business globally. This enables our employees to access IT services from the office or remotely and our customers to access our service offerings instore or online.

Unlike other functions we have the ability to work across departments as the team's capabilities are not limited to IT related projects. We have varying skill sets including Project and Program management, Business Analysis and Quality Assurance.

How can we further support the organisation utilising our current skill base?"

Losses and learnings

Once the business is on an even keel you can pause and reflect. This is the time to look back at how well you led through the change and learn from what went well and what did not. How did your team pull through the change? How did you do? Did you lose talent during the change? If you did what impact did this have overall? What could you have done to reduce the loss of a team member(s)?

Answering these questions will help you become a stronger more proficient leader for when/if another change happens. With the current rate of change it is entirely possible that you will be involved in multiple changes throughout your career. If you work in Information Technology, then it is a foregone conclusion that change will always be on the horizon.

QUANTUM TRANSFORMATION
Mentoring | Coaching | Change Advocacy

LESSONS LEARNT LOG

Step	Function	Lessons Learnt	What event triggered this?	Who is the owner?	Date Occurred	Comments/Learning/ Assessment of Effectiveness
1	Communications	Purpose: To advise of the changes Lesson: Communication during the start of the change needed to be more targeted to the individuals as the messaging got blurred and this caused some disruption in the team.	Updated change plans provided by change champions which were unclear	Manager	15/11/2017	Be certain to discuss mid-stream changes with the change champions to seek clarity. Once changes clear immediately update communications plan and distribute.
2	Structural Changes	Purpose: To provide details on team structure to support the change Lesson: Put the team structure together well in advance of being requested by change champions in order to be prepared for discussions.	Unexpected communication from change champions as to team restructure	Manager	15/11/2017	Be prepared with clear team structure with detailed capability matrix, project schedule and timelines.
3						
4						
5						
6						
7						
8						
9						
10						

For your own development, capture the outcomes of your major actions. This is called a lessons learnt log and is a standard project management tool which helps you to learn from what has taken place. When putting this together during a major change you will want to focus on capturing learnings from each functional area such as Communications, Team Structure, Business as Usual etc.

As with any project, when you revisit what went well and what did not, you will take away valuable learnings that will be useful for the next change you embark upon. The key with any review is to learn from what you have done. It is an opportunity to revisit any actions that you have taken during the change and rework them if you can. Recognising any mistakes you have made and addressing them where you can will help you start with strength in the new organisation.

Reflection is your greatest tool when the change is complete. Looking for areas of improvement will help you develop your own change management skills and process.

Should I stay or should I go?

As "The Clash" so eloquently put it, "Should I stay, or should I go?" Depending on the nature of the change in the organisation you may get to the finish line and decide that it is time for you to move on. This is a valid question to ask yourself—just as your team may have had these thoughts throughout the course of the change—it is natural for you to do so as well. It is not a poor reflection on you as a leader if you choose to leave an organisation that does not help you achieve your career goals. Your answer to this question is entirely personal. It may be time to find your next opportunity armed with your new strong change management skills.

Acknowledge to yourself the great work you have done to get your team through the change in one piece. Know you did the best for your organisation and your team. You have set your team up for the future. They will be fine!

Appendix

Templates for future reference can be sourced from:
https://quantumtransformation.com.au/iop-templates

QUANTUM TRANSFORMATION
Mentoring | Coaching | Change Advocacy

COMMUNICATION PLAN

Step	Who is my audience?	What is the purpose of this communication? What is the message?	What is my supporting material?	Who is the owner?	Target Date	Status	Comments/Learning/ Assessment of Effectiveness
1							
2							
3							
4							
5							
6							
7							
8							
9							
10							

QUANTUM TRANSFORMATION
Mentoring | Coaching | Change Advocacy

CAPABILITY MATRIX

INDIVIDUAL

Role:

Person:

	Below what is required for role	Developing required competency	Appropriate for role	Above what is required for role	At next level
Business Communications					
Customer Service					
Influencing and Negotiating					
Innovation and Creativity					
Presentation Skills					

TEAM

Capabilities appropriate or above

	Person 1	Person 2	Person 3	Person 4	Person 5
Business Communications					
Customer Service					
Influencing and Negotiating					
Innovation and Creativity					
Presentation Skills					

QUANTUM TRANSFORMATION
Mentoring | Coaching | Change Advocacy

TRAINING PLAN

Employee Name: Enter Employee Name Here

Employee Role: Function Manager

Available Courses	0-6 months	6-12 months	12-18 months	18-36 months	Additional Learning	Expected	Booked	Date Booked	Completed	Date Completed	Comments
1.0 Group 1											
1.1 Course Name											
1.2 Course Name											
2.0 Group 2											
2.1 Course Name											
2.2 Course Name											
2.3 Course Name											
2.4 Course Name											
2.5 Course Name											
3.0 Group 3											
3.1 Course Name											
3.2 Course Name											
3.3 Course Name											
3.4 Course Name											
3.5 Course Name											

QUANTUM TRANSFORMATION
Mentoring | Coaching | Change Advocacy

RACI (RESPONSIBLE, ACCOUNTABLE, CONSULTED, INFORMED)

PEOPLE/TEAM

Deliverable									

STAKEHOLDER ENGAGEMENT PLAN

QUANTUM TRANSFORMATION
Mentoring | Coaching | Change Advocacy

	Key Stakeholder (Individual/Group)	What role will they play in the change activity?	How will you engage them?	When will you follow up?	How will you know you've gained their commitment?
1					
2					
3					
4					
5					
6					
7					
8					
9					
10					

QUANTUM TRANSFORMATION
Mentoring | Coaching | Change Advocacy

LESSONS LEARNT LOG

Step	Function	Lessons Learnt	What event triggered this?	Who is the owner?	Date Occurred	Comments/Learning/ Assessment of Effectiveness
1						
2						
3						
4						
5						
6						
7						
8						
9						
10						

Observations

QUANTUM TRANSFORMATION
Mentoring | Coaching | Change Advocacy

As a leader what have you observed about the team behaviours.
List here (try not to have more than 5)

1.
2.
3.
4.
5.

Observations detailed

QUANTUM TRANSFORMATION
Mentoring | Coaching | Change Advocacy

Elaborate on the observations with a sentence for each.

1.
2.
3.
4.
5.

Vision

QUANTUM TRANSFORMATION
Mentoring | Coaching | Change Advocacy

Based on your observations what is our vision to improve the department.

Pillars & Guiding Principles

QUANTUM
TRANSFORMATION
Mentoring | Coaching | Change Advocacy

| *Pillar 1* | *Pillar 2* | *Pillar 3* | *Pillar 4* | *Pillar 5* |

Guiding Principle 1

Guiding Principle 2

Guiding Principle 3

Pillar Detail

QUANTUM
TRANSFORMATION
Mentoring | Coaching | Change Advocacy

Pillar 1
-
-
-
-
-

Pillar 4
-
-
-
-
-

Pillar 2
-
-
-
-
-

Pillar 5
-
-
-
-
-

Pillar 3
-
-
-
-
-

Underpinning Principles Details

QUANTUM
TRANSFORMATION
Mentoring | Coaching | Change Advocacy

Guiding Principle 1:

Guiding Principle 2:

Guiding Principle 3:

Pathway to Success

QUANTUM
TRANSFORMATION
Mentoring | Coaching | Change Advocacy

- *List the ways in which you will succeed in achieving the team vision*

Structured to Succeed

QUANTUM
TRANSFORMATION
Mentoring | Coaching | Change Advocacy

Show your team structure here

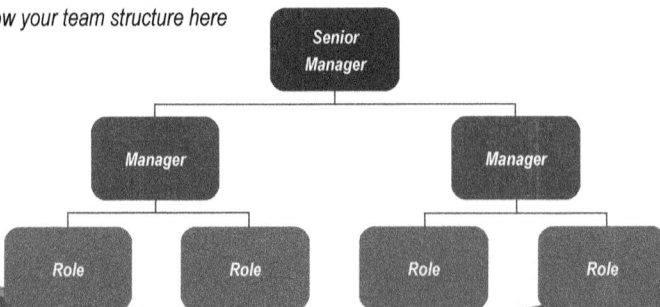

Senior Manager

Manager

Manager

Role

Role

Role

Role

Structured to Succeed Detail

QUANTUM
TRANSFORMATION
Mentoring | Coaching | Change Advocacy

- *Document how this structure will support success*

Measures of Success

QUANTUM
TRANSFORMATION
Mentoring | Coaching | Change Advocacy

Pillar 1	S.M.A.R.T. measure
	S.M.A.R.T. measure
Pillar 2	S.M.A.R.T. measure
	S.M.A.R.T. measure
Pillar 3	S.M.A.R.T. measure
	S.M.A.R.T. measure
	S.M.A.R.T. measure
Pillar 4	S.M.A.R.T. measure
	S.M.A.R.T. measure
Pillar 5	S.M.A.R.T. measure
	S.M.A.R.T. measure

Endnotes

Chapter 1

1. Pohlmann T and Thomas NM (2015) Harvard Business Review – "Relearning the Art of Asking Questions" Retrieved from https://hbr.org/2015/03/relearning-the-art-of-asking-questions [18/12/2019]
2. Ibid.
3. Ibid.
4. Ibid.
5. Ibid.
6. Walker HJ, Armenikis AA, Bernerth JB (2007) "Factors influencing organizational change efforts". An integrative investigation of change content, context, process and individual differences. Journal of Organizational Change. Vol. 20, No. 6, 2007, pp. 761-773
7. Ibid.
8. Ibid.
9. Ibid.
10. Ibid.
11. Ibid.
12. Judge TA, Thoresen CJ, Pucik V and Welbourne TM (1999) "Managerial Coping with Organizational Change: A Dispositional Perspective". Journal of Applied Psychology 1999 Vol.84, No. 1, pp.107-122
13. Ibid.
14. Bordia P and Difonzo N (2009) "Rumors During Organizational Change: A Motivation Analysis". The Psychology of Organizational Change. Viewing Change from the Employee's Perspective. Cambridge University Press 2013
15. Pollack J and Pollack R (2015) "Using Kotter's Eight Stage Process to Manage an Organisational Change Program: Presentation and Practice". Syst Pract Action Res (2015) 28:51-66
16. Kahneman D (2011) "Thinking Fast and Slow". Penguin Press 2011
17. Ibid.
18. Walker HJ, Armenikis AA, Bernerth JB (2007) "Factors influencing organizational change efforts. An integrative investigation of change content, context, process and individual differences". Journal of Organizational Change. Vol. 20, No. 6, 2007, pp. 761-773

19. Ibid.
20. Ibid.

Chapter 2

1. Murphy M (2014) Forbes – "The Status Quo Will Kill Change Management Efforts" retrieved from https://www.forbes.com [15/12/2019]
2. Kahneman D (2011) "Thinking Fast and Slow". Penguin Press Publishing 2011
3. Dobelli R (2013) "The Art of Thinking Clearly ". Harper Publishing 2013
4. Kahneman D (2011) "Thinking Fast and Slow". Penguin Press Publishing 2011
5. Ibid.
6. Ibid.
7. Ibid.
8. Ibid.
9. Ibid.
10. Ibid.
11. Ibid.
12. Ibid.
13. Pollack J and Pollack R (2015) "Using Kotter's Eight Stage Process to Manage an Organisational Change Program: Presentation and Practice". Syst Pract Action Res (2015) 28:51-66
14. Smith I (2006) "Continuing Professional Development and Workplace Learning" – 15 Achieving successful organisational change – do's and don'ts of management. La Trobe University Library Vol.27 No 4/5, 2006
15. Dobelli R (2013) "The Art of Thinking Clearly". Harper Publishing 2013
16. Ibid.

Chapter 3

1. Moran JW and Brightman BK (2000) Leading Organizational Change Vol 12 – Number 2 pp.66-74
2. Kotter J (1995) Model of Change. Retrieved from: https://www.kotterinc.com/8-steps-process-for-leading-change [26/12/2019]
3. <?> Lewin K (1947) Change Model. Retrieved from: https://en.wikipedia.org/wiki/Kurt_Lewin [26/12/2019]
4. Waterman RH and Peters T (1980) McKinsey 7S Framework. Retrieved from: https://en.wikipedia.org/wiki/McKinsey_7S_Framework [26/12/2019]

5. Hiatt J (1996) The Prosci ADKAR Model. Retrieved from: https://www.prosci.com/adkar/adkar-model 26/12/2019

6. Bonebright DA (2010) "Perspectives 40 Years of Storming: A Historical Review of Tuckman's Model of Small Group Development". Human Resources Development International Vol. 13, No. 1, February 2010, 111-120

7. Ibid.

8. Ibid.

9. Ibid.

10. Ibid.

11. Ibid.

12. Ibid.

13. Ibid.

14. Ibid.

15. Ibid.

16. Ibid.

17. Ibid.

18. Retrieved from: https://en.wikipedia.org/wiki/SMART_criteria [19/12/2019]

19. Ibid.

20. Ibid.

21. Ibid.

22. Ibid.

23. Ibid.

24. Ibid.

25. Retrieved from: https://en.wikipedia.org/wiki/Responsibility_assignment_matrix [17/3/2020]

Chapter 4

1. Brockner J, Greenberg J, Brockner A, Bortz J, Davy J and Carter C (1986) "Layoffs, Equity Theory, and Work Performance: Further Evidence of the Impact of Survivor Guilt." Academy of Management Journal 1986 Vol. 29. No.2. 373-384

2. Retrieved from: https://jobs.vic.gov.au [15/3/2020]

3. Ibid.

Chapter 5

1. McGraw PC (2001) "Self Matters". Free Press Publishing 2001

2. Murphy M (2014) Forbes – "The Status Quo Will Kill Change Management Efforts". Retrieved from https://www.forbes.com [12/12/2019]

3. Ibid.

4. Judge TA, Thoresen CJ, Pucik V and Welbourne TM (1999) "Managerial Coping with Organizational Change: A Dispositional Perspective". Journal of Applied Psychology 1999 Vol.84, No. 1, pp.107-122

5. Barnett J (2019) Forbes – "How Managers Can Create an Environment of Psychological Safety". Retrieved from: https://www.forbes.com [19/12/2019]

6. Judge TA, Thoresen CJ, Pucik V and Welbourne TM (1999) "Managerial Coping with Organizational Change: A Dispositional Perspective". Journal of Applied Psychology 1999 Vol.84, No. 1, pp.107-122

7. Smith I (2006) Continuing Professional Development and Workplace Learning – 15 "Achieving Successful Organisational Change – Do's and Don'ts of Management". La Trobe University Library Vol.27 No 4/5, 2006

8. Retrieved from: https://en.wikipedia.org/wiki/Mindfulness [18/01/2020]

9. Retrieved from: https://www.mentalhelp.net/blogs/ocd-and-mindfulness/ [25/04/2020]

10. Williams M (2012) "Mindfulness: A Practical Guide to Finding Peace in a Frantic World". Hachette Digital Publishing 2011

11. Retrieved from: https://www.proflowers.com/blog/practice-gratitude [31/12/2019]

12. Retrieved from: https://www.proflowers.com/blog/practice-gratitude [31/12/2019]

13. Ibid.

14. Ibid.

15. Ibid.

16. Ibid.

17. Forbes Coaches Council (2020) Employee Well-Being Initiatives That Will Boost Engagement and Productivity. Retrieved from: https://www.forbes.com/ [28/01/2020]

18. Ibid.

19. Ibid.

20. Judge TA, Thoresen CJ, Pucik V and Welbourne TM (1999) "Managerial Coping with Organizational Change: A Dispositional Perspective". Journal of Applied Psychology 1999 Vol.84, No. 1, pp.107-122

Chapter 6

1. Retrieved from: https://en.wikipedia.org/wiki/Locus_of_control [29/09/2019]
2. Retrieved from: https://www.axialent.com/busting-silos-four-ways-to-break-down-the-walls-between-us-at-work/ [21/10/2019]
3. Retrieved from: https://tanveernaseer.com/how-to-break-organizational-silos/ [21/1/2019]
4. Kahneman D (2011) "Thinking Fast and Slow". Penguin Press Publishing 2011